SCRIPTED FANTASY IN THE CLASSROOM

ERIC HALL

CAROL HALL

ALISON LEECH

Nichols Publishing

To our parents and partners

First published in 1990
by Routledge
11 New Fetter Lane, London EC4P 4EE

Published in the USA
by Nichols Publishing Company
PO Box 96, New York, NY 10024

© 1990 by Eric Hall, Carol Hall and Alison Leech

Typeset direct from the publisher's media by
NWL Editorial Services, Langport, Somerset TA10 9DG

Printed and bound in Great Britain by
Billings & Sons Limited, Worcester

British Library Cataloguing in Publication Data

Hall, Eric, *1936* –
Scripted Fantasy in the Classroom.
1. Schools. Activities: Drama. Improvisation
I. Title. II. Hall, Carol, *1951* – III. Leech, Alison
792'.028

ISBN 0–415–04811–7
ISBN 0–415–04812–5 (pbk)

Library of Congress Cataloging in Publication Data

Applied for

ISBN 0–89397–370–X

CONTENTS

CONTENTS

ACKNOWLEDGEMENTS

We would like to acknowledge the following people for their unique contributions to this book: Chris Hall, Pete Hall, Jo Delaney, Vanessa and Katherine Jones, Pam Hunt, Nigel Leech, Malcolm Dewell, Maureen McLean, Arthur Wooster and Mick Douglass, and finally Cassie and William, who put up with their parents spending so many hours at the word processor.

INTRODUCTION

We all inhabit a rich, diverse and vivid fantasy world but many of us remain oblivious to the imagery that is continually being generated by our own fertile minds. Just pause for a moment during a monotonous activity such as driving a car or painting a room and reflect on the chain of associations that have surfaced freely during the past few minutes. No doubt you will discover that you have been locked into a changing series of images that seemed to unfold spontaneously. For most of us these images will be predominantly visual, but may also employ the other senses.

In this book, we will suggest how such imagery can be harnessed in creative ways to develop a range of social skills and enhance classroom performance. The benefits that accrue are not normally associated with the fantasy experience. The development of inter-personal skills is central to the process of using fantasy in the class-room. We will show that teachers can increase co-operation, boost self-esteem and promote friendship and respect between students by focusing on scripted fantasy as a legitimate learning experience.

We are primarily concerned with the use of what we shall call scripted fantasy, where after a preliminary relaxation exercise, a series of suggestions are read out to a group of students. The fantasy need not follow a sequential narrative line, although it often has a structural logic all of its own. Within this framework students are free to explore a world of their own imagining and encouraged to communicate its uniqueness to others. The mythology that this is a talent reserved for a few gifted, creative artists needs to be re-assessed. Scripted fantasy is a technique which gives back the im-agination to the individual.

Let us look at the specific educational contexts in which scripted fantasy can be used and the age groups for which activities of this nature are most suited. We have worked with nursery teachers, involved with four- and five-year-olds, who report a high degree of success. Younger children may find it easier to become involved in fantasy because their imaginative capacities have not been dulled by years of experience in schools that emphasise logical, linear and rational thinking, to the detriment of the more creative possibilities of internal processes. Demands for the primary school to address issues such as race, gender and child safety have forced an awareness of the importance of personal and social education on the primary curriculum agenda. We would contend that using scripted fantasy as part of a spectrum of experiential learning methodologies can play an important part in such programmes, by heightening awareness and increasing empathic understanding.

Personal and social education is more commonly associated with the secondary stage of education and is also carried out under a range of different titles such as lifeskills, moral development and health education. Here, too, scripted fantasy is used to add a unique dimension to topics, such as self-esteem, which can lose their impact when dealt with using formal teaching methods or abstract discussion. Similar PSE programmes are now being used with older adolescents on pre-vocational courses in both secondary schools and further education colleges. In these contexts imagery is used to help students rehearse an interview for a job, refuse an unreasonable request or present themselves in a confident manner.

Here at the School of Education, Nottingham University, we have been using scripted fantasy as a technique with mature teachers for facilitating self-exploration and self-understanding for over 15 years. It is essential that teachers experience a scripted fantasy in order to gain insight into the process and share what their students might be going through in the classroom. However, it is also useful for teachers themselves as a form of stress management. It becomes evident that scripted fantasy can be a source of personal, social and professional learning for both teachers and students. Scripted fantasy can also be used for groups of adults with the aim of gaining more insight into their own lives and into how they might change in positive ways. It is becoming a familiar activity in workshops that are designed to foster personal growth.

We would contend that scripted fantasy is not limited only to the PSE curriculum but can be used successfully in a wide variety of educational contexts, provided that the level of vocabulary used in the fantasy script is appropriate to the age and ability of the student group. Imagery techniques seem to work particularly well with special needs students, such as those who do not appear to perform well academically, those whose behaviour causes problems in the institution and students with physical disability. We have even had reports of the successful use of scripted fantasy with students with visual impairment.

In this book we will provide evidence of learning gains, though the exact procedure will need to be varied for different age groups. Clearly, the language will need to be simplified for younger students. There may have to be more preparatory groundwork for groups of students who are unused to responding co-operatively to an adult authority figure. Cynical adults may require a sound rational justification before they are willing to take part in fantasy work. These considerations are explored and strategies for coping with them are offered.

We build up a theoretical framework for fantasy work, while grounding it in practice by providing a wide range of scripts that can be used in the classroom. These are interwoven with the theoretical sections. All of the fantasy scripts and imaging exercises are listed in a separate index for ease of reference.

As a potent illustration, we use the device of a fictional case history to demonstrate the process in the context of a secondary-school classroom and provide a rationale for applications in different subject areas across the curriculum. We go on to offer a psychological analysis of the nature of fantasy, discuss in detail the management and implementation of scripted fantasy work and explore some pitfalls and provisos. An extended discussion of a psychological definition of fantasy is followed by an examination of how imagery can be used in the mental rehearsal of social skills, in improving performance in sport, in healing and for relaxation. We then provide an historical background to the use of fantasy from the turn of the century to the present day. However, the emphasis throughout is on practical ways in which fantasy and imagery can be used to enhance learning from the nursery school to the in-service education of teachers.

Finally, we would encourage teachers to discover for themselves the power and the joy in self-discovery that fantasy can unlock and to share with students the pleasure to be gained from beginning the journey to understand and explore the self.

Chapter One

CASE HISTORY OF A LESSON

Mike Hammond was waiting for his third-year personal and social education class to settle down. He looked around at the faces of the students who came from such varied social and cultural backgrounds and wondered how they would react to the lesson he had planned. Before the students arrived he had put a sheet of paper on each desk and left packs of wax crayons within easy reach.

He reassured himself with the thought that he had already tried out some exercises which had involved relaxation techniques, some aspects of fantasy and drawing, and the students had enjoyed them and asked for more. He felt that the level of personal involvement and the quality of the discussion following these sessions merited a deeper and more concentrated approach. So today he intended to extend the fantasy work. This would mean that the students would have to sit still for quite a long period of time and 3B were not renowned for their ability to be quiet or still.

Mike recognised the importance for himself of establishing an appropriate mental set in trying out something new in the classroom. He understood that being able to tolerate new experiences was an important part of the educational process and that resistance to new ideas was anathema to real learning. He also understood that trying out new methodologies with students in personal and social education might pose a degree of threat or risk for some of them. He had recently attended a personal and social education (PSE) in-service course and had been impressed by the workshop on using scripted fantasy in the classroom. He had felt intrigued enough to read a copy of *Human Relations in Education* (Hall and Hall, 1988), which provided a theoretical framework for experiential learning methodologies, including the use of imagery and fantasy in the classroom. He felt satisfied that from both a theoretical and practical position he was able to calculate the cost-benefits for the students in terms of potential personal learning and felt it was worth the risk. He had read Joyce's (1984) article on the notion of 'dynamic disequilibrium' and had been impressed with the idea that real learning takes place when the individual's world is slightly out of kilter. It is the need to make sense of this 'dynamic disequilibrium' that propels the student towards effective personal learning and can result in either attitudinal or behavioural changes.

As every practising teacher knows, even the best educational theory can go to the wall if the practical management of the classroom is not taken into account. So he had chosen a script which he felt would be suitable for this group. He had even rehearsed reading the script out loud to a colleague in order to assess the speed and tone of his voice. The feedback his colleague had given him had been useful. She had suggested that he speak more slowly and soften the tone slightly in order to produce a more relaxed atmosphere.

> Good morning, everyone. I would like you to settle down quickly today because we are going to do something I'm sure you will enjoy. So Darren, please take your bag off the table because you will need the space in front of you. Shukla, can you sit on your seat ready to begin? Thanks. I must say I have been very impressed with the level of co-operation shown by this group. OK let's get started. Now do you remember the lesson we had a couple of weeks ago when we used some images to help us to relax?... The drawings you did last week are still on the pinboard. Stay in your seats, but just turn round quietly and have a look at your drawing. Now, as you look at the drawing, try to remember what it felt like when you were relaxed.... We are going to try something similar this week but it might take a bit longer.

Mike Hammond knew that it was important to establish a particular atmosphere in the classroom before he began the fantasy. He welcomed the group positively and asked for their co-operation in settling down. He knew that to ask reasonably, giving an explanation for the request, was more likely to prompt a positive response than a negative one. He had learned that it was important to give a group feedback if they did things well when he wanted to enhance their self-esteem and promote a positive group feeling. What Mike Hammond had also learned was that it was his responsibility as a teacher to model appropriate behaviours and that if he wanted to establish trust in a group he had to take the lead in creating a congenial classroom climate.

Directing the students' attention to their drawings helped Mike to focus the group's awareness. This is invariably a quietening process and prepares the students for the lesson to come. They were also asked to recall the sensation of relaxation which is a useful technique for helping to reduce stress levels in any situation.

Before we start, there are a few things I would like to say so I'd like you to listen carefully. As you know, personal and social education lessons are to do with discovering all about ourselves and how we get on with other people. In today's lesson we are going to concentrate on ourselves and the way in which we use our imagination. Once again we will practise our relaxation skills and look at ways of stretching the power of our imaginations. The important thing to recognise is that what comes up for you during the fantasy is uniquely your own – you will have created it for yourself out of your own imagination. After we have gone through the fantasy journey I will show you ways of sharing your experience with others in the group. As I explained to you last time, you have the choice whether to take part or not. If you decide not to take part though, it is important that you don't disturb anyone else in the group. Can I check, is there anyone who does not want to take part?

This stuff is stupid, Sir. Why can't we do proper work?

You're writing this off before you've tried it, Simon. Anyway, if you really don't want to join in, you can sit at the back and read a book on your own, but it is important that you don't disturb any of the others. Would you like to move now, Simon, because everyone else is ready to begin.

Now that Simon has been given a real choice and his decision to opt out has been respected, there is a good chance that he will join in despite himself.

> We will begin by relaxing and settling down as we did last week. Sit comfortably in your chairs. You might like to try and sit up fairly straight, perhaps rest your hands on the table in front of you. Try uncrossing your legs and putting your feet flat on the floor. Just take a few moments to settle down in this position. You might feel more comfortable if you close your eyes.... But you can peep if you want to.... Whatever feels right and comfortable for you. .

Notice that the students have been given a number of choices here. They have been given the choice of whether to join in or not and the choice of whether to close their eyes or not. Offering real choices enables students to begin the process of decision-making and come to terms with taking responsibility for those decisions. It also tends to produce a more positive, co-operative classroom climate because the leadership demonstrated by the teacher is more caring and less authoritarian. It can be further explained to the students that relaxation is an important part of a stress reduction programme which can help them deal more effectively with the stress in their lives – examinations, anxieties about school, personal relationships and so on.

> To start with, try screwing up your face – really tight.... Then let it go.... Now try clenching your fists – really tight.... Then let them go.... Now turn your attention to your breath.... Breathing in.... Breathing out.... Have the sense that your breathing is slowing down.... Now just imagine that you are breathing in warmth and relaxation.... Breathing in relaxation and breathing out tension.... Just relax and let go.... You might hear people shuffling and moving around – or perhaps coughing – but this won't interfere with what you are doing right now.... Breathing in relaxation.... Breathing out tension.

It is important to take the group through a short relaxation before beginning a scripted fantasy. There are a number of different ways to do this. In leading the relaxation and guiding the fantasy, it is helpful if the teacher speaks slowly and in measured tones, allowing the voice to drop at the end of each phrase or sentence. Try not to be put off by students fidgeting or any other noises in the room. The teacher is probably the only person who might be disturbed

7

by them. In fact, any major interruption can be incorporated into the text of the initial relaxation. For example, 'You might be aware of the noise of a class moving down the corridor outside. But this won't bother you as you continue to relax and let go.'

> As we go on with the fantasy, you can choose whether to go along with what I suggest or not and you can stop whenever you want to. Remember that you're in charge of your own experience.

We have dealt with the idea of choice and control earlier and once again stress here the importance of the student taking responsibility for her own experience.

THE PARK

> Imagine that you are by yourself.... It is a warm summer's day and you decide to go to a park.... Perhaps it's a park you know and like or perhaps one you would like to make up in your imagination – anyway, it is a safe place to be.

Virtually any image is potentially threatening. A park could be a place where a student has been frightened by a group of older children or perhaps had an accident. They may even be afraid of being fenced in or of open spaces. Potentially threatening images can be avoided by offering the reassurance that the place is safe and the images are under the student's control.

> You see a bench from which you can see the whole park.... Walk towards it and sit down.... Have a good look around.... Is there a playground in the park?.... Are there swings and roundabouts?.... Are there any people about?.... What are they doing?.... What are the trees like?.... What colours are the leaves?.... Are there any flowers?.... Bushes?.... What else can you see?.... Listen carefully, can you hear any sounds?.... Birds?.... Little children calling out?.... The breeze blowing through the branches of the trees and rustling the leaves?.... Take a deep breath, perhaps you can smell the perfume of the flowers.... Or the recently mown grass.... Feel the gentle breeze against your skin.... The warmth of the sun on your

face.... How do you feel about being in this place at this time?.... How do you feel inside?

Invoking as many senses as possible is a powerful stimulus for both inducing relaxation and generating imagery. Mike used sight, hearing, smell, temperature, touch and internal sensations in this fantasy.

Just as you are relaxing and enjoying the sunshine, the sun disappears behind a cloud.... The breeze becomes stronger and a little chilly.... You can hear the branches and leaves blowing against each other.... As the sky becomes darker you feel a few drops of rain in the air and you realise that if you stay on this bench any longer, you will get caught in the rain.... You get up and run to the trees for shelter as the rain really starts to pour down.... Stand close to the trunk of the tree to avoid the rain and the drips off the leaves.... You reach out and touch the bark of the tree.... How does the bark feel?.... See if you can get your arms round the trunk.... Hug the tree.... Just enjoy the sensation for a moment.

A change of mood could be experienced as the fantasy moves from warm, sunny weather to rainfall. The sense of safety is retained by introducing a safe place to shelter. There is still a strong emphasis on sensory experience, using what may be familiar yet vivid images.

As you turn and lean against the tree, you see someone of your own age, but whom you have never met before, running to shelter with you. As the person comes closer you can see that this is the sort of person that you would like as a friend.... You smile at each other.... Neither of you need to say anything.... You feel comfortable just standing under the tree together.... What does your friend look like?.... Take a few moments.... See how you feel.

This represents a shift from familiar images of nature to the intro-duction of a person and a different emotional reaction may be called into play.

Now you begin a conversation.... What do you say?.... What

does your new friend reply?.... Just let the conversation develop naturally.... Now in imagination, see if you can become
the friend.... What is it like to be the friend?.... As this imaginary friend, is there anything you would like to say?.... What
do you reply?.... Now you realise the rain has stopped and
the sun has come out again.... A clear bright rainbow stands
out against the disappearing bank of clouds.... Together you
walk slowly away from the tree.... You stand in the wet grass
and have a short conversation before you say goodbye to each
other.... Perhaps you arrange to meet again.... Now say goodbye and watch as your friend walks away.... How do you feel
right now?

Taking on the roles in a fantasy, like the friend in the park, provides
a safe way for the student to get in touch with thoughts and feelings
that otherwise may remain unexpressed. The pain of parting is softened by offering the possibility of meeting again.

Have a last look round the park and look forward to the time
when you can return.... Feel the relaxation and the warmth
of the sun as you set off back home.... Now breathe a little
more deeply as you become aware once more of the noises
around you and know that in a moment or two, when you
feel ready, you will open your eyes and come back to the
room.... But don't rush.... Give yourself a good stretch and
when you're ready, open your eyes.

This is a standard procedure to bring people gently out of a fantasy
or relaxation. It is important to do this slowly and sensitively so
that the change between different states of consciousness is not too
abrupt.

Perhaps you might like to sit quietly and just be aware of
how you are feeling right now. (Pause)

The silence following a scripted fantasy can often be cathedral-like
and there is no need to rush a class into activity. Some teachers
find a silence hard to cope with but it is important to be aware of
the quality of a silence before destroying it with an activity. An experiential learning situation like this requires time for silent re-

flection. There are many ways to process the fantasy experience, which we discuss in a later section.

> Now take the sheet of paper in front of you, because what I would like you to do is to draw a part of the fantasy which seemed particularly vivid to you. Make sure you choose colours and textures that express appropriately what you want to draw. Try to be as co-operative as you can about sharing the crayons and pens. You have about ten to fifteen minutes to complete the drawing.

Mike sat silently as the students got on with their drawings and waited until most of them had finished what they wanted to do. He reminded them that they only had a minute or two left to complete the drawings before they were to move on.

> I want you to stop drawing now even if you haven't finished. Please turn your chairs so that you are facing the person sitting next to you. Decide between yourselves who is going to be 'A' and who is going to be 'B'. You are going to take turns in describing to your partner, in as much detail as you can recall, what happened in your fantasy park. 'A's, you will begin. It is very important that as 'A' speaks, 'B' listens carefully to what is being said. Try not to interrupt with details of your own experience; your turn will come. 'B's, just be aware that you are allowing your partner to express what she or he wants to without interruption. You may want to ask her or him a few questions which might help the person to talk in more detail about the experience. But try not to dominate the talking. You will each have five minutes to talk about your fantasy and I will tell you when to change over. Are there any questions?

A common complaint amongst teachers is that students don't know how to listen to each other. We would argue that listening is a skill like any other, which needs practice, feedback and appraisal. Using a focused listening exercise after a fantasy generates a high degree of involvement and curiosity for the students. They want to hear and they want to share, two basic prerequisites if real listening is to take place. Focused listening also encourages a sense of respect

11

for the other person's experience as well as giving the student a chance to talk about her fantasy without interruption. Invariably, practising listening skills in a paired situation like this has a spill-over effect into larger group discussions, where students feel more able to speak and more willing to listen.

Another beneficial spin-off from this exercise is that it encourages students to verbalise a description of a scene using sensory detail as well as a narrative line. Many teachers who encourage creative writing will appreciate the difficulty in stimulating particularly younger students to write using fine descriptive detail. Many teachers with whom we have worked have commented on the improvement in the quality of descriptive writing arising out of the fantasy experience.

> Now you have heard each other's reports of your fantasies, I am going to ask you to reflect back to your partner the main points that you heard. In other words, you are going to demonstrate how skilfully you listened to your partner and how well you are able to summarise the main points of what was said! 'B's will begin. 'A's, don't interrupt as your partner is speaking; you will get a chance to give them some feedback afterwards.

Paying careful attention, reflecting back and summarising are all important social and linguistic skills. By using these techniques in the context of a highly involving but non-threatening activity, the teacher is able to promote these skills in a safe yet structured manner.

> OK, 'B's, your five minutes are up. Now 'A's, tell them how well they did. Concentrate on giving them feedback about the accuracy of what they reported. If they misheard something you said, perhaps you could tell them that too. Remember, all of you, that when you are giving someone feedback you are not blaming them or judging them, but giving them information about how well you think they performed a particular job.

The ability to give and receive feedback is another highly important social skill. Here students are given the opportunity to hear a relatively unbiased appraisal from their peers.

> Is there anything anyone would like to say to the whole class about what you have done this morning? You don't have to put your hands up to speak, but take it in turns and try to allow people to finish what they have to say before you make your own point.

The language here is soft and gentle and in keeping with the fantasy activity. No one has been coerced into doing anything and the options have been left open.

Several of the students talked about their experience, including Jane, who had never volunteered before to speak in front of the class. The group appeared to listen attentively and seemed genuinely interested in what others had to say.

Teachers have often reported that the discussion following a fantasy is involving for the whole class. Students appear to be listening and sometimes students who are withdrawn in other situations will volunteer to speak. Their contributions are respected; the students seem to recognise the authenticity of each report.

Mike was surprised when the bell went. He thanked them for working so hard and looked forward to seeing them next lesson. The students drifted out slowly and quietly to go to their next lesson; some were reluctant to go. Others went up to Mike and said how much they had enjoyed what they had done. Mike felt that the lesson had been a positively rewarding experience for him as a teacher because he felt the students had gained a great deal from the lesson in terms of both their personal and academic development.

Later, during the lunch break, Mike sat down with a cup of coffee in the staffroom. John Forster, 3B's form tutor, came across to join him.

> John: I'd like a word with you, Mike. Sarah Smallwood, who is in my form, was chatting to me over lunch about what you were doing in your PSE lesson this morning. I wasn't at all sure I liked what I heard. I wouldn't like the parents to think you've been 'hypnotising' their children. I hear you do very good work in PSE, but...

13

Mike: I'm not too sure what you're saying. Did Sarah say that she felt she was being hypnotised?

John: Well, she didn't exactly use that word, but to be quite frank with you, Mike, I got the impression that some of the children had got upset about what you had done. I heard that some of them went very quiet and behaved oddly.

Mike: What do you mean, 'oddly'?

John: You know, out of character. I will give you an example. Frank Timms, who normally races around all lunchtime, was sitting quietly in the form room when I went in for registration!

Mike: That doesn't seem a serious problem to me.

John: Look, our job isn't to meddle with the children's personalities. Leave the therapy to the educational psychologist. We don't want to get splashed all over the Sunday papers!

Mike: All I did was to take them through a short script of a fantasy. I got the impression that they enjoyed it. They were keen to try some more.

Margaret Walker, who taught French, leaned over and joined in the conversation.

Margaret: Are you talking about 3B? What on earth did you do to them this morning? I've never known them to be so quiet and co-operative. I asked them what they were doing in the previous lesson but they were very secretive about it. All I could get out of them was something about looking at pictures in their minds. Very intriguing.

Mike: Oh, I was trying some fantasy work with them. It seemed to go extremely well. I'm surprised that the effects went on into the next lesson. Mind you, they did seem pretty relaxed.

Margaret: I'm still not clear what you did, but if it has this kind of effect on 3B, I might try it too. What exactly does it involve?

Mike: Well, I got them to relax in their chairs, we've done this before, and then read them a script about going to a park and meeting a friend.

Margaret: It sounds like telling them a story.

Mike: Yes, in a sense. Only I just give them a few ideas and they fill in the details. As each one of them is doing it for themselves, they get really involved.

These are typical of some of the issues that may be raised by colleagues about the use of scripted fantasy in the classroom. The suggestion is sometimes made that personal material of deep psychological significance is being raised in the students and that it requires the help of a skilled professional to handle the outcome. Certainly, the images that emerge may be important to the students but usually they are very happy to have undergone the experience and are able to draw their own conclusions from it. As we shall argue later, having others give interpretations of imagery, like the standard Freudian symbology, or having the teacher tell students the meaning of their experience, is potentially harmful. A 'real' expert is unlikely to indulge in these activities.

We have had feedback from several hundred teachers on the outcomes of using scripted fantasy with many classes. Out of the thousands of students involved, there have been no reports suggesting psychological damage and no complaints from parents regarding the activity.

There is a strange, almost irrational element in the suggestion sometimes made, that this 'sort of thing' should not be done if there is even the remotest possibility of harming one student. We would agree if we thought this might be the case. However, there is a wealth of educational research which shows that countless numbers of students have had their self-concepts irreparably damaged by poor teaching in traditional subjects. So it seems that indulging in even the most conventional school activities is potentially damaging. The sports field is another place where there is a risk of real damage to students – players regularly injure themselves. One of the authors broke his neck playing rugby and another is maths phobic after eleven years of traditional maths teaching. These risks seem to be accepted by the educational establishment with equanimity and we have heard no demands for either maths or rugby to be removed from the timetable. It is worth repeating that we have had no reports of psychological damage to students as a result of taking part in scripted fantasy, or of complaints from parents.

Anxieties about hypnotism are also commonly expressed. These are based on misconceptions about hypnotism. If a person is relaxed, there is a good chance that she will be in a mild hypnotic state and might be amenable to suggestions that are made to her. But it must be emphasised that this is happening a great deal of the time in normal, everyday communication. Skilled communicators have always exploited this suggestibility to their advantage, either consciously or unconsciously. The forms of scripted fantasy we are offering here put the responsibility for generating the exact content of the imagery squarely with the individual student. This compares favourably with the insidious control of internal processes exerted by, say, the advertising industry.

Some students take a long time to come out of the fantasy experience, sitting very still for a few moments after the others, with their eyes closed. This need not be a cause for concern; it is a normal post-relaxation phenomenon. There may have been issues raised or insights gained which the students would like to stay with for a while. If an individual student stays in this state for a longer period of time than seems appropriate, a gentle squeeze on the wrist will quickly bring her back to the room.

We have presented here some of the misgivings that we have heard expressed about the use of scripted fantasy in the classroom and will be dealing with these issues in greater depth in subsequent chapters. Let us turn now to list briefly some of the educational benefits that we believe accrue from such an activity:

1. The acquisition of basic relaxation techniques as part of an ongoing stress reduction programme in PSE or PSHE.
2. The development of listening skills.

3. The valuing and respecting of other students' contributions.
4. The creation of a co-operative and friendly classroom climate with the concomitant benefits of enhanced self-esteem and more self-responsible classroom management.
5. The acquisition of a wider repertoire of writing styles.
6. The acquisition of a wider vocabulary to express the subtleties and nuances of feeling and emotional states, giving the student access to greater self-expression.
7. The development of oral skills. The ability to express clearly and concisely aspects of personal experience and to make meaningful interpretations of that experience. The ability to give a verbal response to unpredictable questions.
8. Increased levels of creativity and skill in art work.
9. Increased self-awareness.

This is undoubtedly an impressive list, but we do not intend to give the impression that the classroom teacher should not be careful with the introduction of techniques of this nature to students. Problems could be generated by teachers who are not particularly well-adjusted emotionally. However, it is likely that the same teacher will also be involved in problem situations that do not involve fantasy and the real issue is whether the person concerned has chosen the right profession or needs to be given more support in the institution.

There is no doubt that the use of scripted fantasy in the classroom will generate a range of feeling states in the students. They may become quiet and reflective, they may become sad or even cry, they may become excited and energized.

It is the acceptance of the feelings of sadness, hurt, grief and even despair that some teachers have difficulty in handling in themselves or their students. This anxiety in the face of the expression of emotion is something that many of us have learned in our various cultures, but this same repression of feeling is now understood to be both emotionally and physically damaging. If you are shocked by the expression of feelings in others, particularly students, then the use of scripted fantasy is not for you. Certainly there is no evidence to show that the expression of these feelings is bad for the students. If anything, the opposite is the case and the sharing of feelings enables students and teachers to come together as a more cohesive and caring group.

It is important that the teacher should experience the process of going through a fantasy in a group setting and that she should have gone through it several times using a range of themes. There are three main reasons for doing this. First, it provides the teacher with an understanding of the state of consciousness involved. Second, it demonstrates the unique quality of each person's imagery. Third, it provides the teacher with a fund of experience which can be shared with students. This is summed up by an experienced English teacher who had been introduced to scripted fantasy on the M.Ed. in Human Relations at Nottingham University: 'As experience enabled me to reject my prejudices against imagery and fantasy, I now needed experience to allay my fears and uncertainties about using imagery with students.'

If, after having experienced a scripted fantasy, you feel that your response was predominantly negative towards the activity, or doubt your own ability to introduce it to a group of students, then it would be better to leave it aside for the moment. In making the decision about whether or not to use scripted fantasy in your classroom, it is also important to consider whether you will be able to cope sensitively with the feelings that the students may experience and report. Strong feelings are likely to be generated when the main theme of the fantasy is to do with self-exploration and where issues linked with the self-image are being examined. The teacher should try to appraise honestly her own ability to handle what emerges from such an exploration. If the self-appraisal throws up a reluctance to take on such a role, then again we would suggest that work on scripted fantasy be temporarily postponed.

CURRICULUM APPLICATIONS

The example we have discussed in this chapter is concerned with self-exploration and would fit neatly into a PSE programme. There are, however, very potent applications for scripted fantasy across the curriculum.

English, language and literature, is an area of the curriculum that has much in common with the ideals, aims and methodologies of PSE. As we have mentioned earlier, English teaching is clearly an area where fantasy can be used as a stimulus for creative writing, poetry or prose. We would not claim this to be innovative but we offer illustrations and give examples of practical outcomes later in the book. One of the writers, a former English teacher, used fantasy as a stimulus for discussion, developing awareness of intrinsic creativity, building up a feeling vocabulary and even as a way into exploring set texts for examination syllabuses. Working with students from the ages of 11 to 18, fantasy was a successful and essential part of the teaching repertoire for a subject which is concerned at a fundamental level with self-expression. Many of the scripts in this book were used in this context.

Art and design, like English, are concerned with forms of self-expression, but through different media. We would suggest that drawing is a particularly potent method of processing fantasies and many teachers have commented on the improved quality of students' art work following the fantasy experience. The stimulus for this improvement seems to lie in the ability of the fantasy to tap feelings that may be difficult to express verbally but find a vehicle through drawing. One nine-year-old graphically expressed this notion after having completed a drawing of her fantasy tree: 'There aren't enough words to describe feelings. Pictures say more.'

Dance, music and drama are also curriculum areas that demand a greater feeling response from the student. Fantasy has a long and honourable history of being used in the expressive arts as a way of drawing from wells of creativity. Fantasy can be used to extend empathy so that characterisation can be more readily entered into. The relaxation generated by fantasy is likely to provide a means to bypass blocks to creativity.

This same unblocking process may play an important part in physical education. Many PE teachers complain that mental attitude is often a block to physical performance and fantasy may provide a methodology to release some of the blocks. Fantasy has been seen by some athletes and their trainers as a way to hone up skills and specific techniques and improve performance. Borrowing from techniques used by professional sportswomen and men we discuss these applications in more depth in the chapter on the right brain.

GCSE history syllabuses underline the need for students to acquire the skill of empathy and many teachers are finding that they need to extend their own repertoire of teaching techniques in order to achieve this aim. With the use of appropriate scripted fantasy material, this could be a realisable goal. Similarly, geography students could be encouraged to enter imaginatively into different cultures, landscapes and living environments. Geographers teaching physical geography could employ the fantasies 'Exploring a River' and 'Climbing a Mountain', perhaps modified to introduce specific features, for example, glaciation. Students from urban environments could be asked to journey in their imagination to rural scenes; rural students could be asked to do the reverse. Discrepancies between the students' fantasies and examples of photographic reality could be discussion points. This type of work could also be extended to examine the validity of cross-cultural stereotypes, which largely exist at the fantasy level.

One of the writers (Jones, 1986, now Leech) offers an exemplary model of the use of fantasy in Religious Education. However, great care has to be taken in this area not to elevate students' responses to the fantasy to the level of a religious or spiritual experience. We would argue that becoming more in tune with feelings is in itself a precious gift but one which is under the control of the fantasiser to bestow upon herself. Hall (1987) discusses the associated difficulties in this area.

Science and maths in schools are traditionally areas that are linked with rational, linear left-brain thinking. A superficial analysis would suggest that scripted fantasy has nothing to offer these disciplines. We would want to suggest a contrary view, that using scripted fantasy can serve as a useful complement to the more accepted teaching styles and a way of extending the students' mathematical and scientific thinking into a more intuitive mode. The greatest mathematicians and scientists, from Leonardo da Vinci to Albert Einstein, have combined intuitive and rational thinking modes to powerful effect (Capra, 1982).

Students find maths and science difficult areas because many of the concepts are presented abstractly and many of the processes remain invisible. It is this fundamental detachment of the student from the experience which seems to render her incapable of making general inferences from the learning. What scripted fantasy can offer is a bridge between the abstraction – the process out there – and the student's ability to grasp the essence of the concept through the use of imagery. When this is combined with the pure enjoyment of the fantasy experience, a difficult piece of scientific process can become transformed into real experiential learning.

Below is an example of this bridging process at work in a science lesson. This script provides an analogy for the condition of molecules of water as they change from solid ice to liquid water and then to water vapour as a gas. It would be helpful for the teacher to provide an initial preamble about the structure of molecules of water and how they change with temperature and to then concretise this using the following fantasy script.

ICE, WATER, WATER VAPOUR

Close your eyes and relax in your chairs.... Perhaps take a couple of deep breaths.... Begin to feel more relaxed as you let the tension go.... Now imagine that you are a molecule of water.... You can look like anything you want to.... Just go along with what comes up.... But now I want you to imagine that the other students in the class are also molecules of water.... Be aware that the temperature is becoming very cold.... Extremely cold.... So cold that you are unable to move.... Like a block of ice.... Fixed in your chairs.... Now the temperature is starting to rise.... Feel yourself loosening up.... Movement returning.... In a moment, the bell will go for breaktime and all the molecules in the school will start to move.... Move like water.... Now the bell goes and all you molecules are set free.... In the corridors, in the play-ground.... Moving like water.... All held together within the school, but all moving freely.... Be aware of yourself as a molecule of water moving towards other molecules and then moving away.... Be aware that the temperature is rising again.... Much hotter than before.... Now the bell goes for home-time and you find yourself as a molecule of water moving through the school gates on your way home.... You are now free of all the other molecules.... You can go wherever you like.... Spreading out in all directions away from the school.

The second example involves the creative use of fantasy, but without the need for a script or for closing the eyes. In scientific terms it provides insight into the work of a catalyst in the Haber process, which combines nitrogen and hydrogen to form ammonia, but it also provides an exciting, stimulating learning environment for the student. This particular lesson was devised by a science teacher in his initial year of teaching.

CATALYST

The teacher drew an enormous test-tube on the floor and said, 'Imagine the girls are molecules of nitrogen and the boys are molecules of hydrogen. I would like you all to go into the test-tube.' Predictably, the boys and girls stayed separate from each other. 'Right, I am the catalyst platinum,' said the teacher as he took the hands of one boy and one girl and joined them together. He continued to do this until every boy was holding hands with a girl. 'Right! Now you have formed ammonia and you could not have done it without me.'

Some of the fine detail of the process has been omitted here, such as the fact that the operation only takes place at high temperatures and that a simple test-tube would not be adequate. However, the event is likely to be remembered many years later and, we hope, the chemical process with which it was linked. Much of the content of conventional science lessons is quickly forgotten. As we shall suggest later, this imaging experience is still recalled, like some dreams, years later.

What used to be called home economics, now food technology, can also usefully employ these fantasy techniques. Fantasy can be used first as a means of exploring the chemical processes involved in the science of food, for example the use of egg white as a raising agent, and second, as a means to explore feelings about nutrition and bodily health. The fantasy 'The Healthy Body' might be a stimulus for discussion about how health can be optimally maintained by sound eating habits. More science examples, on batteries and bulbs and on metamorphosis, can be found in Johnson (1978).

Forms of imagery can also be used to enhance understanding of mathematical concepts. Here we quote in full from Maureen McLean, a secondary school maths teacher, who used imagery to revise the mathematical properties of the circle with a group of students.

CIRCLE

Use of imagery came about quite inadvertently the first time I used it. It was the last two lessons of the day. I was trying to revise 'The Circle' with my 'good' fifth year group. There I was, standing at the blackboard, chalk in hand, giving 100 per cent of the last of my energies to try to drive home the necessary information. There they were, sitting, for the most part, with half-glazed expressions on their faces. Suddenly something inside me either snapped or clicked.

I left the blackboard, sat down and told them to close their eyes. Immediately the half-glazed looks disappeared; they were interested.

I began by asking them to draw a circle in their minds. We examined the shape, identified the fact that no matter which way we turned it there was always an axis of symmetry from top to bottom. This led us to see that there are an infinite number of axes of symmetry.

Using the technique of getting them to draw the circle in their minds, by adding chosen points, joining points, creating angles, moving lines (and most importantly seeing the lines in our heads), we managed to cover every geometric property of the circle. The response was terrific. Instead of half-hearted responses from a few braver members of the group, just about everyone replied when asked if they could 'see'. Their faces became animated – some even smiling!

As an example of the response, I wanted them to move a chord down through the circle to see that the property of the line from the centre of the circle meeting a bisected chord at right angles applies to a tangent. As they were slowly moving the chord down through their circles, one of the students shouted out excitedly that the line was 'sticking out' of the circle.

It seems ridiculous to me now that I had not thought of doing this before. Mathematical concepts and their application cannot be learned off by heart – they need to be 'seen' to be understood and the birthplace of ideas and understanding is in our minds. So what better place to start the teaching of maths, than in the mind?

The activity of 'seeing' mathematical concepts may not suit all students and some of them may have trouble visualising anything. However, it may be that through the device of the fantasy students are better able to identify for themselves sticking points in their own learning process. It does seem in this anecdotal account that a high proportion of the class was gaining a great deal from this activity. It may be that the outcomes reported here are the product of the motivation generated by a novel activity and if the process were repeated for every lesson the effects would wear off. Our guess is that the techniques are very robust in relation to this inhibition effect.

Maureen McLean developed the use of imagery further in maths lessons by pausing briefly during the explanation of a difficult concept and suggesting, 'Just close your eyes and try to see it.' This only took a few seconds but the students appeared to have no difficulty in following the procedure and they commented that it was a useful device to help them grasp the concept.

Modern language teaching lends itself to mental rehearsal. Nowadays the emphasis is on teaching vocabulary within specific contexts: the restaurant, the airport, the shop and so on. Students are asked essentially to role-play the parts of diner, passenger and customer with the ability to converse effectively in the target language. They are then asked to demonstrate publicly, usually to the teacher's satisfaction, their verbal skills in these situations. Many students find this a frighteningly difficult task and are frozen by their fear of speaking in public, even if they have retained the vocabulary. Using visualisation techniques to rehearse mentally the vocabulary within a given context can help overcome their fear. The suggestions can be offered in the instructions given to the students that the mental rehearsal be done confidently, with good humour, and that it is alright to make a mistake. This internal rehearsal, designed for students to experience the positive feelings of success, will probably increase the chances of an enhanced performance in the public situation. Such techniques can be modified creatively to fit in a programme of language teaching designed to improve the students' spoken ability in the target language.

The use of imagery and relaxation in language teaching is not a new development and forms part of the system called *Suggestopaedia* developed in Bulgaria by Lozanov. For language teachers who require a fuller description of this system, we would recommend *Superlearning* by Ostrander and Schroeder (1979).

Fantasy can be used particularly effectively with students who have special educational needs. There is a wide range and diversity of students who are defined in this way. Although there are specific difficulties to overcome in relation to some disabilities, we know of many teachers who are actively involved in overcoming the barriers. For students with hearing impairment, fantasies can be done with eyes open and the instructions signed. Even students who have been blind from birth appear to be able to respond to a scripted fantasy in a way that is meaningful for them. In both of these instances teachers are enabled to enter the students' phenomenal world in a unique way and therefore have a better understanding of their emotional lives.

Effective communication is a characteristic difficulty for students with special educational needs who remain in the mainstream. Poor self-image, lack of confidence and learned helplessness all contribute to silencing many students or, conversely, to acting out and disruptive behaviour. Fantasy is by definition a non-competitive activity; each individual's fantasy is unique and can be shared and valued in its own right. The possibility of making invidious comparisons is lessened and gradually less confident students can be encouraged to share their experiences and thus begin the long, hard process of rebuilding their self-esteem. As fantasy does not have to be processed through writing – drawing and talking are equally effective – students who have negative feelings about writing will not be discouraged. Indeed, teachers may find that students want to write about their fantasy experience because it is a highly motivating activity.

In later chapters we discuss the importance of mental rehearsal for students with severe learning difficulties, but again this is a valuable adjunct to all special-needs teaching. Many students are encouraged to go out into the 'real' world and try things out for themselves, to increase their sense of independence and control over their own lives. Getting a bus into town, following directions, making a phone call and obtaining a drink from a vending machine are all examples of situations that could be mentally rehearsed beforehand. Emotional dependence and dependent behaviour can be an acute problem that can be exacerbated by the school environment. Mental rehearsal provides a taste of success and the feelings that accompany independent behaviour. Discussion of the rehearsal may enable students to disclose ambivalent feelings about dependence and independence which they may not have addressed directly before or indeed even been aware of.

The introduction of the national curriculum in the United Kingdom has sharpened the existing dividing lines between subject areas. Paradoxically, many educators acknowledge that these divisions are at best a management strategy, at worst an unnecessary constriction that closes off possibilities for learning. Scripted fantasy is an educational tool, both cognitive and affective, which cuts across the subject divide. It can be used to great effect with all ages and all abilities. What is required of the teacher is the flexibility and creativity to modify scripts to suit her particular educational goals and the courage to try using a teaching style that may require relating to students in a more open, honest and caring way.

Chapter Two

CATCHING AN ELUSIVE CONCEPT

It would be rare to find scripted fantasy being introduced as a methodology in any initial teacher training course, so the procedure described in the previous section of guiding a group through a fantasy may be one with which you are unfamiliar. Over the last few years, however, with the introduction of PSE into the school curriculum, fantasy work is becoming more commonplace in the classroom and is now accepted as part of a repertoire of skills that teachers use to enhance the process of self-awareness and personal growth in their students. From our observations, though, it is both teachers and students who report that taking part in the activity provides a powerful learning experience.

In this chapter we will define fantasy within the context of current psychological thinking and distinguish it from other forms of imagery in order to extend the reader's theoretical background and understanding of the concept.

So, what exactly was happening in Mike Hammond's classroom?

IMAGERY OR FANTASY?

It seems likely that aspects of imagery and fantasy were being evoked by the procedure and that the experience was quite different for each student. We would include in this the teacher who was reading the fantasy script. The terms 'imagery' and 'fantasy' are often used as if they were interchangeable, although to be precise, all fantasy includes imagery, but not all imagery includes fantasy. If you were were to summon up a memory image of an apple, it would probably not include any elements of fantasy.

As a term, imagery tends to be used in a broader sense than fantasy and refers to:

1. an internal representation of a perception of the external world in the absence of that external experience;
2. an internal representation that is unlike any previous experience you have had.

Compare the previous example of the apple with an image of a fairy castle in a far-off land. The second image will probably have more 'fantastic' elements in it.

Fantasy tends to be used to describe a sequence of internal events that are neither representations of external reality nor controlled in the rational, conscious sense. Images frequently emerge and flow in forms that are non-linear, perhaps altogether different from everyday experience. Perceptions of time may be collapsed or extended and temporal sequences distorted. This definition would apply to the experience the students in Mike Hammond's classroom went through. It is also impossible to control directly or alter the course of another person's fantasy from the outside and this leads to problems in educational institutions where thought control, not learning, may be the real goal of the activity.

Thus the word 'fantasy' has often come to be used in a derogatory sense. Teachers do not usually encourage students to 'indulge' in fantasy. Daydreaming is frowned upon and linear rational thinking is rewarded. It is no coincidence that the current Secretary of State for Education has made a strong statement about the reintroduction of learning maths tables by heart. Teachers may be able to control external behaviour but not what is going on in the students' minds. Part of the anxiety may be the fear that all fantasy is either sexual or escapist. Teachers, like other adults, may be afraid to examine their own fantasy life for this reason and thus extend this restriction to students. This is part of a generalised distaste for introspection, which in a highly materialistic society is construed as a somewhat eccentric self-indulgence.

The word 'imagery' is used more positively. It is connected with the imagination which teachers are supposed to encourage. Imagination may result in products, such as a poem or a painting, that are seen as legitimate educational activities and are open to assessment by the teacher.

Despite the poor press that fantasy has traditionally received, there is no doubt that it can be harnessed to improve academic and social performance, such as in the mental rehearsal for an impending interview or by improving the quality of creative writing. This positive, constructive use of fantasy has until recently been ignored in education. Other disciplines, however, have been quicker to appreciate its potential and we will go on to show in a later chapter how fantasy has been used creatively in both sport and medicine.

FANTASY AND REALITY

Although we have been using terms like 'internal' and 'external' world, the difference between fantasy and reality is not always clear. In the psychological laboratory, several subjects failed to distinguish between an object they were asked to imagine and a picture of the same object (Perky, 1910). They were asked to summon up an image of a banana on a blank screen in front of them. An image of a banana was then projected onto the back of the screen. Some of the subjects thought that the projected image was the one that they had imagined.

Sometimes we 'see' a projection of how we wish the external world to be, rather than what is really there. In the case of mistaken identity, we often see the person we were expecting to see and, realising the mistake, the features actually change in front of us. Teachers and students may distort their perceptions of each other on the basis of their expectations, fantasies and previous experience in just the same way.

These are indeed complex philosophical issues and while we would not claim to have any easy answers to the fantasy/reality debate, we would say that by training students to pay more attention to and extend their fantasy lives in a creative but controlled way, it may help them to have a clearer grasp of what the differences between fantasy and reality mean for them.

USING THE SENSES

Individual reports of imagery tend to be described in visual terms, a description of what can be seen 'in the mind's eye'. Imagery can, however, involve any of the senses: hearing, taste, smell, touch, balance, hot, cold, and pain, as well as sight. People vary as to which sense they emphasise, and feel more comfortable with. Bandler and Grinder (1979) distinguish between people who are predominantly 'visual', 'auditory' or 'kinaesthetic' – seeing, hearing and feeling. After a fantasy, students will give reports of their experience through their preferred mode of expression.

If the teacher is aware of how the students are using language, then a response can be made with reference to the same sense, such as, 'What else did you see/hear/feel?' Students working in pairs can also be encouraged to listen for these modes and to respond appropriately. They can also be encouraged to widen their repertoire of response by using sensory modalities with which they are less familiar.

This use of language can emerge in more subtle ways, again reflecting the unconscious preferences of the speakers:

- 'I see what you mean', implies a visual preference.
- 'It sounds very strange', implies an auditory preference.
- 'I feel that I can understand the image', implies a kinaesthetic preference.

Some people would claim that they move easily between the three modalities (and others too) and it would prove an interesting exercise to try to demonstrate this empirically.

The more senses that are included in the fantasy script, the greater the chance that most of the students will become involved and that individuals will have a more meaningful experience. At the same time, practice in the non-preferred senses extends the students' abilities to resonate with the external world. This use of the senses was clearly illustrated in the script in the previous section.

VIVIDNESS OF IMAGERY

David Hume, the eighteenth-century philosopher, suggested that images had less 'force and vivacity' than normal 'sensations, passions and emotions', implying that images are fainter than sensory experience. This may have been the case for Hume, but it is not necessarily true for everyone. Some people inhabit a rich fantasy world. This may be a way of compensating for the drabness of a humdrum existence, though it is equally possible to have a rich external life as well as a rich inner life. It may be that Hume, by emphasising the use of rational thinking, diminished his own imaginative capacities.

Galton, the nineteenth-century psychologist, tested eminent scientists on their ability to summon up an image of their breakfast table. Many of them reported experiencing no visual imagery at all. This sort of self-report is fraught with problems. Psychologists have asked people to rate the vividness of their imagery, but there is no way of comparing the ratings of different individuals. A person who claims to be experiencing vivid imagery may, in reality (whatever that means), be having fainter images than someone who is being more modest. In this instance at least, comparisons appear to be odious.

In spite of the problems of self-report, it is likely that there are differences in the quality of imagery that individuals experience. Again, Galton's scientists could have diminished the more fanciful capabilities of their minds by an excessive use of logical and rational thinking, a process that is probably being repeated in most conventional education at all ages. It is interesting that some exceptionally innovative scientific discoveries have been made in a state of dreaming or reverie. Kekule, a nineteenth-century, chemist came to the understanding that organic molecules like benzine are closed rings or loops following a dream of snakes swallowing their tails. Jerome Singer, one of the few psychologists to study imagery seriously, reports having rich visual imagery throughout his life, which may explain the motivation for the direction of his research (Singer, 1974).

FORMS OF IMAGERY

Which forms of imagery are we concerned with here? Let us first deal with forms of imagery that are not our prime concern, though aspects of these forms may be present during a scripted fantasy. These would include:

1. *After-imagery.* This is produced by staring at a well-lit object for a period of time and then shifting the gaze to a blank surface. The resultant after-image is probably due to lingering activity in the retina. This is best illustrated by staring at an illuminated light bulb for a few seconds and then looking at a wall or sheet of paper.
2. *Eidetic imagery.* This is the ability to look at a complex visual

scene and then be able to 'see' it in the 'mind's eye' and describe it in fine detail, as if the eye were a camera photographing a scene. This ability is largely limited to young children and people living in non-technological societies. Some formally educated adults retain this ability in the form of a photographic memory, which has obvious advantages in examinations.

3. *Memory imagery.* This is quite simply remembering events from the past. Unlike the photographic quality of eidetic imagery, when we try to remember events from the past, for most of us it tends to be a much vaguer experience. Inevitably, some memory images will be involved in the content of a fantasy.

4. *Daydreaming.* We are all familiar with this activity, though we may feel guilty about it and even deny its existence. This is not just an indulgence of the idle adolescent, but, as reports by Singer (1966) suggest, it is something we all do most of the time, even when we are performing complex intellectual tasks.

5. *Hypnogogic and hypnopompic imagery.* These are respectively, the images that come into consciousness as we are falling asleep or waking up.

6. *Dreaming.* We all appear to dream but the reports concerning the quality of dreams vary tremendously. We do not intend to deal with dreaming in this book, though some individuals experience a scripted fantasy as being dream-like. For most people however, it is clearly different.

7. *Hallucinations and perceptual deprivation imagery.* If an individual's sensory experience is limited in some way, perhaps as part of a psychological experiment, under torture or brainwashing, or even performing a monotonous task, then images may be produced spontaneously. It is as if the nervous system needs to produce visual, auditory and tactile hallucinations in order to make up for the deficit. Try spending long periods of time with the eyes closed, as in sitting meditation and similar forms of imagery are likely to emerge. Psychiatrists will be familiar with the unbidden images that force themselves into the consciousness of some disturbed people, for example, schizophrenics.

The types of imagery described in these last four categories, daydreams, hypnogogic and hypnopompic imagery, dreams and hallucinations, tend to be passive experiences in the sense that they are not consciously controlled. The images just seem to emerge, flooding in in often very idiosyncratic ways, but this does not mean that the imagery is serving an unimportant function. Simply paying attention to your daydreams is likely to reveal themes that may be important in your life, either by highlighting recurrent patterns of behaviour or by meeting unfulfilled needs that are not being satisfied by everyday existence.

SCRIPTED FANTASIES AND GUIDED FANTASIES

In contrast to the previous categories, the two categories below involve procedures that invite the fantasiser to pay close attention to the content of the imagery and to have some degree of control over the total process. In this way, the fantasiser takes a much more active role in the creation of the fantasy.

1. *Scripted fantasy*. The central theme of this book is the educational implications and applications of scripted fantasy. It is important to differentiate between scripted fantasy and guided fantasy as the two terms are often confused. Here we use the term 'scripted fantasy' to mean a situation in which a prepared script is read to an individual or a group, as a stimulus for a fantasy journey. The scripts might cover any one of a variety of themes but have been written to avoid prescribing the responses from the fantasiser. In this way, the feelings, senses, people and places will be the fantasiser's own. The individual or the group would normally be relaxed with their eyes closed.
2. *Guided fantasy*. In a guided fantasy, an individual is also relaxed, with eyes closed. A second person, usually called the guide, offers a broad theme to initiate a fantasy journey. Examples might include: climbing a mountain, following a stream from its source down to the sea or a search for a precious object. The person who is undergoing the fantasy journey reports the experience aloud as the images unfold. The guide helps the fantasy along in a way that extends the report and encourages the person to examine aspects of the fantasy in a non-directive, non-interpretive manner. It is a one-to-one technique and thus generally unsuitable for the

classroom, but it can be used in a counselling situation. The term 'guided fantasy' is often used to describe a scripted fantasy. For the purposes of this book, we will use the terms as we have defined them here.

Although for the purpose of more accurately defining the term 'scripted fantasy' we appear to have separated it from the other types of imagery, there is no doubt that these other types are called into play to some degree during a scripted fantasy. It is unlikely, however, that after-imagery is involved. Some students fall asleep and dream, while others drift off into extended daydreams that have no connection with the script.

In our experience, most students report scripted fantasy as being a unique experience and claim that they are involved in a state of consciousness that they have not encountered previously. The students usually feel relaxed and yet quite alert. The fantasy tends to generate feeling states that may be seen as either positive or negative but nevertheless appear to be safe. Students have described being both involved in the fantasy while at the same time being a detached observer. This dual awareness permits them to break out of the fantasy at any time. Only a small minority of students deny having any imagery at all and their imaging ability tends to improve with practice. It is not uncommon for the experience to be described as extraordinary.

As we suggest in a later chapter, these linked processes of imagery, relaxation and feeling are sometimes described as 'right brain' activities. These processes are contrasted with rational thinking, which is mediated by the left brain. Physiological psychologists now suggest that this model is too simple. However, personal reports do suggest that there are two separate sets of activities and that involvement in one precludes the other. 'Left brain' activity has been encouraged in our culture to the neglect of 'right brain' activity, but we would suggest that it is time that teachers began to offer students a more balanced, holistic education.

Chapter Three

TURNING FANTASY INTO A REALITY: THE MANAGEMENT OF SCRIPTED FANTASY IN THE CLASSROOM

PREPARING THE ROOM

In an ideal world an empty, carpeted room or a room with easy chairs would make a superb setting for introducing scripted fantasy to a group of students. Carpeted rooms are available in some schools and it may be worth making an effort to find out what facilities there are in your institution. We are familiar with schools that have carpets in a television room, a barn-like sports area and in the well of a lecture area. Primary schools, even if they are open-plan, often have a carpeted quiet room.

It is worth planning ahead to locate the best physical setting for the group you intend to work with. Moving to a new room will set up the expectation that something different is going to happen and the students are likely to appreciate that you have made an effort on their behalf. The reason for chosing a carpeted room is to allow the students to lie down for the relaxation, so that maximum benefit is derived from the process. This can create its own problems though, particularly for older students who may find lying on the floor embarrassing. You need to use your judgement about this. Moving to a specialised room can provide the privacy required for this kind of work. If other students or staff are able to look in the windows, it can be unsettling for both you and the group. The simplest solution, if a move is impractical, is to draw the blinds or curtains. Privacy is a very important issue and one that should be considered carefully before beginning fantasy work with a group.

Let us start with the less congenial situation: the standard classroom, with rows of desks and chairs, no carpets and no curtains. This is the situation most teachers have to put up with but this need not be a barrier to successful work in this area. We know of one teacher who turned the desks to the wall and this strategy seemed to work very well. Once the fantasy has got under way or after students have completed a few fantasies, the physical setting will cease to be so important. This is one of the many paradoxes thrown up by working with fantasy.

Make sure that the room is comfortably warm, not too hot and reasonably draught-free. The lighting of a room can be problematic. If you turn the lights off with a naive group, this may cause an unnecessary distraction. Other members of staff may even be discomforted by it. Certainly turning the lights off may increase a sense of relaxation but there seems little guarantee that it will improve the quality of the imagery. The optimal situation is a quiet, stress-free environment, although we are aware this is not always possible to find in schools.

TEACHER PREPARATION

Homework

In Chapter One, 'Case History of a Lesson', Mike Hammond provided the consummate model for the preparation of a lesson involving fantasy. We all know that the reality in schools often does not measure up to the ideal. Nevertheless, we would offer a word of warning. One of the writers borrowed a script without first reading it through thoroughly and it proved totally inadequate for the group concerned. We would not advise others to fall into the same trap.

It is important then to read more than just the title of a script. Don't assume that the script will meet your requirements until you have read it beforehand. If it is the first time you have tried using a particular fantasy script, read it aloud and ask for some feedback from a friend on the pace and tone of your delivery. The script should be read in a relatively neutral and non-threatening tone of voice. Try to keep the voice gentle and avoid the temptation to be over-dramatic, or emphasise particular words or phrases. The reading of the script should provide the students with an emotionally clean slate to work on.

In the classroom

We would not encourage teachers to try out scripted fantasy in the

36

spirit of 'Let's fill in an empty slot'. The fantasy scripts could be seen as an end in themselves as in the context of a Personal and Social Education course, in which students are encouraged to think about who and what they are and share feelings with others. Alternatively, the fantasy may be used as a tool for enhancing cognitive learning across the curriculum. Thus in a science lesson fantasy might be used to help students remember the parts of a flower or the internal workings of a bodily organ. Either way, some preparation will be necessary. So check that:

1. Intellectually, you are aware of the rationale behind introducing the fantasy as part of the learning process.
2. Professionally, you have structured the lesson so that the students are clear about the aims, methods and evaluation of the exercise.
3. Physically, you allow yourself to take part in the relaxation. Reading the instructions for relaxation can be relaxing in its own right.
4. Emotionally, you accept that you might feel anxious if it is the first time that you have used fantasy in the classroom.

PREPARING THE MATERIALS

If the fantasy experience is to be processed through drawing as opposed to poetry or prose, then the teacher will need to have a selection of different-sized paper available for the students' use. This may seem like a small point but in fact there may be some learning just in the size of paper a student uses to express her fantasy imagery. Once again the teacher models the notion of offering students a choice here, the optimal spatial context for self-expression. This also applies to the use of drawing materials: felt tips for strong bold expression, wax crayons and pastels for a more subtle, muted line. We would suggest that these notions could be introduced to the students via an instruction such as: 'Choose the size of paper that feels appropriate to express how you feel right now. Try to pick colours and textures that really show an image or picture from your fantasy.'

Mike Hammond laid out the paper and a selection of crayons on the desks before the lesson began. Although this is a convenient way of managing the activity because it minimises movement and possible disruption in the period immediately following the fantasy, it does reduce the possibility of choice. Experienced teachers are likely to find little difficulty in combining maximum choice with minimal disruption.

PREPARING THE STUDENTS

You have prepared yourself, the script and the room. How do you prepare the students? Three main aspects need to be considered:

Intellectual preparation

It is important to introduce the lesson with a short discussion of the purpose of the activity. We gave an example of this in the previous chapter, where the fantasy was fitted into the context of a series of lessons in Personal and Social Education. Apart from the obvious good manners of explaining to students what you intend to do, it is necessary so that students can make a real choice of whether to take part or not. They cannot make a responsible choice without information, but if it is to be a real choice, arrangements have to made to cope with students who opt out.

Emotional preparation

Some students may be fearful of doing something different. This may be expressed in what is often called 'bad behaviour': giggling, deriding the activity, talking loudly and making demands to go back to a more conventional lesson. This latter demand is usually made by those who co-operate least in conventional lessons. A response to this kind of behaviour can be to say explicitly what is going on:

> I can understand that you are a bit nervous about this as you have not done it before. But if you want to, just go along with it and see how it feels to try out something new.

This kind of response demonstrates acceptance of what the student may be feeling while at the same time encouraging them to be more adventurous.

Another aspect of this reassurance is to make it clear, as Mike

Hammond did, that the students do not have to take part. It is, however, equally important to make it clear that those who opt out must not interfere with the others. This might prove a source of difficulty as the teacher cannot ensure the enforcement of this injunction. Certainly in the context of a PSE lesson, the teacher might look at the issue of group responsibility in terms of providing an opportunity for each member to do what they want without sabotaging the educational agenda.

It also needs to be pointed out that the students can stop participating in the fantasy at any time. All they have to do is to open their eyes. Another choice that helps to allay their fears is whether they have their eyes open or closed. Oaklander's (1978) phrase, 'You can peep if you want to', puts the student in a double bind. If students close their eyes, they are co-operating with the activity. If they 'peep', then they are also following your instructions. This may appear to be somewhat manipulative but we would suggest that it is a benign form of manipulation.

Physical preparation

How to sit

In our view, the optimal position to sit for scripted fantasy is in an upright position. Some teachers prefer students to put their heads on folded arms on the desks. This may remind them of their infant school days, which probably carries many comforting memories. However, leaning forward can constrict the breathing and students may be more likely to fall asleep.

We would suggest the following set of instructions:

> Make yourselves as comfortable as you can. Shuffle around a bit first and then try to sit with a reasonably straight back. It might help to sit well back in the chair. Make sure your legs are uncrossed and your feet flat on the floor as this will help you to relax. Place your hands on the desk or in your lap.

There is a distinct possibility that some students will not follow these instructions but there is little point in insisting. You may find that they will move towards your suggestions in future sessions having gone through the procedure once. An alternative technique would be to allow the students to relax in any way that felt comfortable for them; then slowly, over a number of sessions, build in the more correct relaxation posture.

How to relax

Once the students are sitting in a reasonable position and the shuffles have subsided, you can help them to relax further. Scripts related to relaxation are included in a later section but we offer a brief example here:

> Just be aware of how you are sitting in the chair right now.... You may notice that there are parts of your body that are feeling tense.... Just check now to see if there are any areas of tension.... I am going to give you a few suggestions about how to relax a little more and I would like you to try to follow my instructions.... Begin by clenching your fists really tightly.... Now let them go.... Next I want you curl your toes under really tightly.... Now let them go and relax.... Hunch your shoulders up to your ears.... When you let them go, relax the shoulders and the neck.... Be aware of how you are feeling in your body right now.

This type of exercise points up the difference in bodily feeling between tension and relaxation and serves as a good introduction to relaxation procedures. However, don't relax the group too much. If you extend the time spent on relaxation you may find that some students will fall asleep. Once the group becomes more accustomed to the procedures for introducing a fantasy, a few short instructions for relaxation will probably suffice. This is a matter of intuitive judgement on the part of the teacher.

Paying attention to breathing can also be an aid to relaxation. You might like to try out these instructions:

> Be aware of your breathing.... Is it fast or slow?.... Easy or forced?.... Shallow or deep?.... Try to let the breath deepen.... Breathe deeply down into your chest.... As you relax and let go.... Enjoy the feeling of relaxation as it flows all over your body.

Eyes open or closed?

We have twice referred to the question of whether the eyes should be open or closed during the fantasy. Some students find classrooms very threatening places and seem frightened to close their eyes as a result. There are others for whom closing the eyes signals a loss of control and therefore becomes an anxiety-provoking experience. This can also be true for adults. It is certainly not helpful to force the issue and insist that students close their eyes. Only by going through the fantasy will they be able to trust that the experience is a safe one. Even with eyes open many students and some adults can have a vivid fantasy experience. For those for whom closing the eyes is a difficult instruction but who are anxious to conform to the teacher's requests, the suggestion, 'You can peep if you want to', allows them to do just that.

Timing

The amount of time spent on reading the scripted fantasy to a group of students depends upon the pace of the individual's delivery. In our experience most of the scripts that we offer in this book take between ten to fifteen minutes to read aloud. A minimum of fifteen minutes is what we would advocate for the drawing of any aspect of a fantasy. When working in pairs, to process the experience verbally we would suggest between five and ten minutes for each student. For some this will seem like an inordinately long period of time; for others it will have merely begun. Either way, the teacher must be prepared to renegotiate these time boundaries if they seem inappropriate to the level of concentration or motivation of the group. However you decide to carve up the time, bear in mind the total process consists of: introduction, relaxation, fantasy, processing and whole group discussion to share the experience.

Other aspects of timing would include: when in the term you introduce fantasy work, how often and what proportion of a programme of work it should take up. It would be nice to wave an authoritative wand and provide glib answers for these questions but it would be irresponsible to suggest that anyone other than the members of a course-planning team could make these sorts of decisions with any degree of competence.

Age

Much of the discussion so far has centred on the needs of young adolescents – secondary school students. The same management

41

considerations apply to adults, including teachers on in-service courses. It is strange how mature adults will present the same 'discipline' problems as school students when they are placed in the situation themselves. They will insist that a slumped position is the most comfortable and ignore suggestions to the contrary. They find it difficult, even embarrassing, to close their eyes and, like the youngsters, need to be offered the suggestion, 'You can peep if you want to'. An equal proportion of adults and adolescents have difficulty in closing their eyes and will look round suspiciously to see what the others are doing. Some will even attempt to sabotage the session by asking questions once the script has been started in order to distract the facilitator from carrying out the task. It is useful to remind the group in this instance that the task is optional. Opting out, though, should not be interpreted as meaning the disruption of the entire group.

At the opposite end of the age range, two of the writers have used short fantasies to calm their three-year-old child and to induce relaxation prior to sleep – with varying degrees of success, it must be admitted, although we put this down to resisting the 'facilitator'. Delaney (1988) provides a fascinating account of the use of scripted fantasy with a vertically grouped infant class and has also used the technique successfully with nursery children. Delaney makes three important observations about working with very young children.

First, she found that the same fantasy script can be used again and again and still generate a high degree of involvement. This partially overcomes the problem of the paucity of relevant material for this age group. Second, she found that scripts that have a surreal element to them, such as some of those in De Mille's (1976) *Put Your Mother on the Ceiling*, were particularly effective. The younger children did not find the bizarre imagery a barrier to their imagining in the way that older students and adults often do. Third, there was a higher level of what might be construed as 'disruption', with the infant children responding as if they were watching a television screen. They chortled aloud, gave running commentaries, exclaimed loudly when exciting images popped into their heads and even pointed to parts of the imagery with their eyes closed. Generally they took a much more uninhibited, active part in the process. This type of response has been extinguished by the time they reach secondary school, usually as a result of negative feedback from teachers. This is not intended to be a condemnation of teachers handling large groups of children. We recognise that a fundamental part of the socialisation process is about deferring gratification and learning appropriate behaviour in groups, but we would argue that this need not entail stifling creativity.

Caveat

Many teachers find that using scripted fantasy with students is a highly successful activity in that it improves the quality of relationships, reduces stress and produces work of a high quality. Nevertheless, try not to be seduced into overkill. Although the experience bears repetition, this should be done within the context of a planned programme of work, not, as we have mentioned before, as a 'slot filler'.

PROCESSING

Processing a scripted fantasy enables students to make sense of and reflect on their immediate experience, as well as providing the opportunity to relate this to past life experiences. Processing should be an integral part of the fantasy experience, for without the chance to reflect on and share with others the symbolic meaning of their fantasies, students miss a rare opportunity to glimpse both the uniqueness and commonality of human experience.

There are many ways in which the students can report back their experience. Talking, writing, drawing, dancing and musical composition are just some examples.

Talking

At the end of a fantasy the students will probably be fairly quiet for a while, as a result both of the relaxation and the fantasy itself. This is the natural result of a highly introspective activity so there is no need to feel anxious about this. Try going along with the atmosphere in the room. Don't hurry the students into activity.

When the class is ready, they can be invited to form small groups, preferably pairs, to talk about their fantasies. It is best to start with pairs until the students have learned to listen and wait for their turn to speak. Groups of three provide a wider range of experiences to share, but some students find it difficult to hold on to their own material while others are relating theirs. Once a group is practised in working this way and have begun to understand what co-operative behaviour entails, they can be encouraged to work in larger groups.

Invite the students to decide who is to speak first and give them a specific time to speak so that no individual dominates the discussion. The task should be clearly and simply stated. For example:

> I want you to describe in detail what happened in your fantasy. Try to bring the scenes to life for your partner and say how you felt as you go along. If you are the person who is listening, try not to interrupt with material from your own experience. You will have your own turn soon. Your task is to concentrate your attention on your partner and to encourage her to explain the experience in as much detail as possible. If she forgets to tell you about her feelings, you might ask, 'How did you feel about that?'

After the discussion about the fantasies you might invite the groups to spend five minutes reflecting on how well they performed the task of listening to each other. In this way, students receive direct feedback on their ability to focus their attention on someone else in a caring, sensitive manner. If the opportunity to do this is provided routinely, then small resentments can be expressed and appreciations voiced. This minimises the possibility of undercurrents of bad feeling building up in a group and contributes towards building a positive classroom climate.

This way of relating to a class is very different from conventional teacher behaviour, since it gives far more control to the students over their learning. For the teacher who is unused to small group work, it can be unsettling not knowing exactly what has been taking place, in case the groups are not on task. This feeling is linked to a loss of power, status and control. Conventionally, secondary teachers particularly are in a powerful position to influence a whole group's learning. Giving up centre-stage and looking on from the wings might be a painful process for teachers used to the attention of an audience, even if the audience is a captive one.

From our own experience, though, fantasy generates a high degree of involvement with the task and time-wasting is not an issue. Confirmation that the groups have been working on the task can come towards the end of the lesson as a result of asking: 'Is there anything anyone would like to share about their fantasies with the whole class?' Invariably, several students will want to talk in front of everyone. This is one of the few times in a school day that the whole class will be involved in and listening to a discussion.

Listening skills exercises

The skills of listening can be enhanced with specific exercises. Here are three listening exercises to practise in pairs: ˜

1. Ask the students to choose a partner. If this normally generates a lot of noise, ask them to do it non-verbally. Instruct the
   pairs to divide up into 'A's and 'B's. Ask the 'A's to talk for
   about three minutes on a given topic. Ensure that the subject
   is an emotionally involving one, for example: 'My earliest
   childhood memories'. 'B's task is to listen without making any
   verbal contribution and at the end of the three minutes repeat the main points of what has been said as accurately as
   she can. The 'A's can then provide feedback on how well the
   'B's performed the task. Ask them to swap over and repeat
   the exercise.
2. This exercise allows students to feel the difference between attention and inattention. Again, ask the group to form pairs
   and divide up into 'A's and 'B's. Have prepared a set of written instructions for each of the 'B's. Ask the 'B's not to show
   their partners the sheet. The instructions should make it
   clear that the 'B's are to avoid eye contact while the 'A's are
   talking. After two minutes, direct the 'B's to make eye contact
   and lean slightly forward in their chairs. While the 'B's are
   following these instructions, the 'A's are to talk for about six
   minutes on: 'The worst thing about being my age is....' At the
   end of the exercise, invite the 'A's to guess what the secret instructions were. Then ask them to discuss how they felt during the six minutes and if they noticed any differences in
   their partner's behaviour. If they did notice differences, 'A's
   should comment on the effect the differences had on them
   and how they made them feel. Then reverse roles and repeat
   the exercise even though the 'A's know what the instructions
   are.
3. Ask the group to choose a partner and decide who will be 'A'

and who will be 'B'. Instruct the 'A's to talk for approximately three minutes on: 'What I would really like to change about my behaviour is ....' While the 'A's are talking, the 'B's have to listen attentively to their partner and, *when appropriate*, only ask the question: 'How do you feel about that?' At the end of the exercise ask the pair to discuss the effect that the question had on the quality of the discussion.

Teacher's response

It would be clearly inappropriate if teachers were not to model effective listening skills for students. Work in social skills training demonstrates the importance of the modelling process for the effective transference of skills from the trainer to the trainee. We would suggest that it is crucial that teachers model listening skills at all times but especially when students are reporting their fantasies to the whole class. The following example may serve to clarify this point and we will return to the fantasy used in the 'Case History of a Lesson' of a visit to a park.

> Teacher: Where would you like to begin in describing your fantasy?
> Student: Well, I've got a picture of the tree in my mind.... and it told me that it was friendly and would look after me.
> Teacher: So your tree told you that it liked you and would take care of you?
> Student: Yes, I knew I wouldn't come to any harm when I was next to the tree.
> Teacher: What were your feelings towards the tree?
> Student: I felt as though I wanted to hold it.
> Teacher: How were you feeling inside?
> Student: I felt really warm inside and wanted to go to sleep.
> Teacher: What do you like about being asleep?

In this short extract the teacher first demonstrates reflecting back the content of what the student has said and then moves on to encourage the student to make statements of feeling. These techniques help the student say more about the nature of her experience. The questions follow closely what the student has said and avoid the danger of the teacher manipulating the content of the student's own material.

Questions that manipulate the introduction of new content are less helpful and in our view can be very destructive. At this point it might be useful to talk more specifically about modes of questioning. A distinction is often made between 'open' and 'closed' questions (Hall and Hall, 1988), that is, a question that opens up communication or closes it down. In the short extract of dialogue above, each question invited the possibility of a variety of responses from monosyllabic to effusive – the choice being the respondent's.

Avoid questioning in the following ways:

1. 'Did you think the tree was friendly?'

Superficially, this may sound reasonable but unless the student has already used the construct 'friendly' to describe the tree, then it is an inappropriate intervention. The danger here is that the student might accept it just because the teacher has said it. The power dynamic inherent in the teacher/student relationship makes it imperative that the teacher use only material introduced by the student and avoid projecting her own feelings indiscriminately. We will discuss this notion of projection in a later chapter. Therefore, avoid the kind of question that invites the students to follow a way determined by the teacher. The teacher needs to try to suspend her own feeling agenda in order to hear exactly what the student is saying. In this way the teacher demonstrates that she values the student, and that she values hearing what the student has to say. One of the spin-offs of real listening by the teacher is the enhancement of the student's self-esteem. We would maintain that this is a vital first step if students are to be encouraged to value themselves and their own experience.

2. 'Why did you feel warm inside?'

This question invites the students to talk about their motives and reasons. Many students are unaware of their motives. To talk about the reasons for feelings is not appropriate in this context. If students want to make connections with their own lives or pursue their reasons and motives for specific behaviour during their fantasy, then they can do this at the moment when it feels right for them and not when it feels right for the questioner to make the connection for them. Those readers who are acquainted with or work in the area of counselling will recognise an overlap in terms of the skills being used. However, a sharp distinction should be made between the process of counselling and being talked through a fantasy experience in the classroom. Students have patently not contracted into a therapeutic relationship, even if elements of this may develop. They would have every right to feel aggrieved if they were probed by a teacher in front of a group of their peers. A gross example of probing would be: 'Did you need the tree's friendship because you haven't many friends of your own?'

A feeling of being probed is often induced by 'why' questions. Questions that begin with this word are often felt to imply some sort of covert moral judgement by the respondent. For the questioner it is rather like saying, 'I don't feel warm inside, so why should you?' A common response from students to 'why' questions is to say 'I don't know', which is probably an accurate response. Alternatively, they might give a jokey, cynical reply to an interrogatory style of questioning from a teacher. In general, a useful guideline is to avoid using questions beginning with 'why' when talking about personal experience.

3. 'Why didn't you want to climb the tree?'

This question is a redirection of the discussion and may again reflect what the teacher would like to have done herself. It also carries a covert criticism of the student's experience and in this way subtly undermines self-esteem. The student may deny her own feelings just to 'please the teacher'.

If pitfalls such as the ones outlined in the three examples given above are avoided, then something rare may take place. During a dialogue between teacher and student, information and statements of feeling begin to flow in the opposite direction – that is, from student to teacher. The skill of the teacher is to encourage the student to elaborate on her initial statements without judging or misrepresenting them. In this way the teacher becomes a mirror to the student, reflecting without distorting the images. This process promotes a deeper understanding of the self while the self that may be revealed meets with acceptance within the context that it is being explored, for example, a PSE lesson.

Writing

'Writing up' is the common form of processing experience in the classroom. All students will be familiar with the business of listening to a story or going on a visit and then having to write about it. You may be familiar with the cartoon in which one student is saying to another, 'Don't look out of the window or the teacher will tell you to write about it!' Used in this way, writing becomes a chore and not an activity that has intrinsic enjoyment. Curiously, students are usually eager to write about their fantasies and, as we will show later, use more complex language and express feelings more sensitively. Some children may prefer to write in the form of poetry rather than prose and this option can be given before the writing starts.

It is useful to encourage students to use the first person, that is the pronoun 'I', and to write in the present tense. They are writing as if the events of the fantasy are happening at that moment in time. This prevents them from distancing themselves from the experience and enables them to write with a power and immediacy that is often missing from students' writing. The very act of committing the events of their fantasy to paper enables them to own their own experience and reflect upon it.

Much conventional education involves telling students what their experience should have been and the correct manner in which it should be reported. The writers recall, with not a little distaste, how writing in the passive voice was drilled into us in science lessons as a way of recording experiments. If the work is not reported in an acceptable way, then it runs the risk of being rejected. This is particularly true for special needs students, who may find it difficult to understand what the teacher expects of them. For all students, writing about scripted fantasy can be a highly personal experience and for teachers concerned with evaluation it is important to develop a method of assessment that is appropriate to the emotional content of the work. The teacher has to accept that the students have a right to express their own experience in the way that feels appropriate to them. We are not arguing here for a neglect of the conventional writing skills but we are suggesting that PSE lessons need not have these particular skills as their main priority. These skills already assume a inordinately large proportion of the curriculum in most schools and yet, ironically, standards are still claimed to be in need of improvement.

Some of the statements in the last paragraph may seem to some commonsense, to others downright polemical. Nevertheless, we would argue that this kind of work demands a high level of respect for the individuality of the student and upon this fundamental principal we base our philosophy.

Drawing

It's hard to talk about your feelings but you can draw how
you feel. It doesn't get rid of the feelings, but it helps a bit.
(a nine-year-old girl)

Fantasy can be processed using any of the expressive arts: dance, modelling with clay or plasticine, drama, music, human sculpting, mime and so on. We will limit our comments to drawing, the medium that is most used in the classroom and most convenient to organise.

Drawing may require a change in the way you use the limited funds that are available for resources. It is helpful to have a plentiful supply of different qualities of paper, ranging from rolls of lining paper to cartridge paper. If you ask round the school or college you may find sources of paper that are not being used. A supply of good wax crayons or thick felt tip pens will be appreciated by the students and encourage more expressive drawing. Conventional coloured crayons, which many students own, are more limited. As a last resort, in a time of financial strictures, it is possible to ask students to do drawings in an exercise or rough book, perhaps to accompany a piece of writing.

Older students and adults are sometimes inhibited about drawing and in our experience even dread the idea. Perhaps this is because they associate drawing with the achievement of a set standard rather than with enjoyment and self-expression. It is important to stress that artistic merit is of no importance for the purposes of this activity. Even so there may be individuals who are frightened by the prospect of drawing in public. A way round this is to invite the whole group to draw with their 'other' hand, the non-dominant hand. This can release inhibition for everyone – after all, no one is expected to draw well under these conditions. In reality some 'other' hand drawings turn out to be unexpectedly expressive. The quality of drawings produced in this way might, as we suggest later, be explained by the split-brain hypothesis.

If you intend to use drawing following a fantasy, it is less disruptive to have the paper and crayons available beforehand. However, allowing students to choose the type and size of paper and texture and colour of drawing materials encourages self-expression. There is no need to rush the students into activity and you need to judge intuitively when to give the instructions. Ten minutes might suffice for a drawing, a time limit which also releases students from the idea that they have to end up with a perfect production.

Displaying art work produced out of a fantasy is a means whereby students can share their experience with the whole group. From our experience, looking at a display of fantasy drawings produces a whole variety of emotional responses in students, something that does not necessarily occur when they are looking at work produced in conventional art lessons. Curiosity, amusement, wonder, sometimes awe, sadness and empathy are emotions that often surface. This engagement in each other's work on a feeling level can only serve to foster appreciation of art in a wider context.

CONFIDENTIALITY

The processing of fantasy in the classroom may encourage students to make personal statements with a degree of feeling in both content and expression. This raises the important subject of confidentiality, an issue for which many teachers would like a hard and fast rule. An example of this might be the edict: 'Everything that is said in this room is confidential and must not be repeated outside'. The somewhat simplistic notion that such a thing is possible reflects both the insecurity that many teachers working within the affective domain may feel about handling personal issues that come up, and the more serious business of a failure to address the central issues, psychological and cultural, concerning confidentiality. In intrapsychic terms, the teacher who has difficulty handling self-disclosures in the classroom may also have problems self-disclosing herself. Culturally, the inability of an institution to handle sensitively the twin issues of self-disclosure and confidentiality may be an accurate reflection of the value a patriarchal society places upon the expression of feeling. This is an extension of the ostrich syndrome – if as educators we collude with the pretence that feelings don't exist, then maybe we won't have to deal with them. Looked at in this way we can begin to see that there is a much broader issue at stake here, which is not unique to the experience of processing fantasy work. It is part of the hidden curriculum of a school in which trusting and caring relationships between all members of the institution often have an unfortunately low currency and even lower priority.

We would argue that the expression of feeling and other forms of self-disclosure have a legitimate place in the school curriculum, as legitimate as maths, French, computer science and so on. In this way, confidentiality becomes an issue not to be avoided, but to be placed in its correct perspective. It is possible for teachers to create problems by over-emphasising confidentiality. It is as if talking about feelings were so unusual in schools that we have to have strict rules to handle it. Thus confidentiality may be re-interpreted by students and other teaching colleagues as secrecy, and secret activities often carry connotations of guilt, embarrassment or even shame. Students and their teachers have a right to confidentiality if that is what is required to help them to begin the process of talking about themselves and their experiences in a real way. Enforcing or policing this right emerges not out of teacher edicts but out of an awareness of what it means to respect the needs of each other. It is a group issue and can profitably be presented as such by the classroom teacher.

To begin the group discussion the teacher could model making her own needs in relation to confidentiality clear at the outset:

> I don't mind if anyone shares anything I say outside the classroom, but if there is something specific that I say which I would rather remain with us as a group, then I will ask you to keep it confidential. Although I will do my best to respect anything you say in confidence to me, there are times in my role as a teacher when it might be impossible to keep a confidence. If it would help I could talk a little bit more about the times when it would be difficult for me to respect a confidence and why [give examples]. I guess that some of you might find the same difficulty keeping a confidence in your role as friend. Working with a partner, discuss possible situations in which you would find keeping a confidence difficult and why.

Most students have very efficient censoring mechanisms and if they are not being pressurized, they will only reveal what feels appropriate to them. Certainly it is important to make it clear that students do not have to talk or write about any aspect of their fantasy experience that they prefer not to, but to over-emphasise this invites the conclusion that the content of the fantasy will be difficult to share and that they will need to be secretive about it.

The solutions lie in the behaviour of the teacher. By following the guidelines set out in this book, problems related to confidentiality are unlikely to surface. Words and phrases like 'suggest', 'invite', 'whatever is right for you' can soften what might be heard as an injunction from the teacher to self-disclose. When students are sharing in smaller groups the suggestion can be made that students should make a clear statement to the other members of the subgroup if they do not want what they have said to go any further. By and large, the opposite is the case, in that scripted fantasy provides a safe means for the students to talk about their feelings and their personal lives and they are grateful for the opportunity to do so.

Chapter Four

INTRODUCTORY SCRIPTS

The following set of scripts are designed for introducing a group of any age or ability to scripted fantasy. They are based upon situations with which the majority of students will be able to identify, and encourage a mixture of memory imagery and fantasy.

There is nothing sacred about the exact wording of any particular script and although the vocabulary may have to be adjusted to suit the age and experience of the group you are working with, don't be afraid to write your own scripts.

WRITING YOUR OWN SCRIPT

If you intend to write your own scripts, be careful not to manipulate the wording so that the group is forced to work through issues that are important to you. For example, if the expression of anger is difficult for you, don't be tempted to exclude the possibility of that emotion emerging out of the script. However, avoid using the students to work through your own unresolved feelings of anger. This is not to say that feelings should be discouraged but that specific feelings need not be prescribed by the text. Using the open question in the script: 'How are you feeling right now?' precludes the possibility of emotional manipulation.

It is essential that you do not introduce frightening or shocking images when students are in a suggestible state. It may not be helpful to ask students to face their own deaths, for example, or to have a meeting with God. Existential questions about the nature and purpose of existence may emerge out of a fantasy experience but this must remain under the control of the student. Let us unwrap this point further. A script is presented with death as the main theme. The group has little choice in avoiding what must inevitably be a very painful experience. If, however, they were to be presented with a script whose main theme was a train journey, quite clearly some students may interpret the journey as a symbolic one between life and death, while others may experience it as merely a pleasant interlude from the routine of daily existence. Whatever interpretation the individual makes, it is her choice. The probability is that whatever interpretation is made, will be the one that the student is capable of handling emotionally at that point in her life.

Such problems can be avoided by using broad open themes. If there is an animal in the fantasy, then permit the students to choose the animal. If there are to be any words spoken, allow the students to choose the words. Allow the maximum freedom to the student while still permitting the general theme of the fantasy to unfold. Maximising the students' freedom of choice within the broad theme of the fantasy reduces the possibility of resistance and increases the opportunity for the students to explore their own issues freely.

INTRODUCTORY SCRIPTS

It can be argued that students need to be trained to image before they can move on to a more extended fantasy script. There are exercises designed to develop the imaging capacity. For example, the student might be asked to image a triangle, then change the colour of the triangle or even change it into a square. We would suggest that exercises of this nature are far more difficult than following a simple story line and the degree of student involvement in the task is noticeably lower. The manipulation of deliberately constructed images may be a useful learning experience but we would not consider it to be a prerequisite to successful imaging in a more extended form.

A useful way of drawing students into a scripted fantasy is to include suggestions that involve attending to sensory experience, particularly at the beginning. Certainly most of the scripts in this book model this approach. An aspect of sensory data often neglected is the internal emotional state – feelings and moods. Attending to sensory data may block normal rational thinking and encourage imagery. Either one of these processes appears to inhibit the other. The first script we offer concentrates almost entirely on sense data.

BONFIRE NIGHT

This fantasy will appeal to students of all ages and abilities. For older students it may invoke pleasant memories of childhood and the excitement that bonfire night inevitably engenders. It has been designed to take the student through the five main senses. Afterwards, they can be asked which sensory modality proved to be the most vivid for them.

Take two breaths and allow your body to relax.... Just let the tension go.... I want you to imagine that it is bonfire night.... Where are you right now?.... There is a big bonfire with bright yellow flames leaping up to the dark night sky.... Can you see a Guy Fawkes on the top?.... See the light flickering on the faces of the other people around you.... Take a good look at them, who are they?.... Watch the colours of the fireworks as they flash and sparkle.

Listen to the sounds of the fireworks.... The zooming rockets and the loud bangs.... Hear the crackle of the fire as it burns and collapses into itself.... Listen to the excited shouts of the children as they call to one another.... Can you hear what they are saying?

Feel the warmth of the fire on the side of your face.... The sharp cold of the November night air on the other side.... Feel your feet and wriggle them around in your shoes or boots.... Are your feet warm or cold?.... How are you feeling inside?.... How do you feel about being here?

Breathe in the smell of the burning fireworks.... Sparklers are being lit.... Take a deep breath and smell the burning sparklers.... Someone is cooking some potatoes and sausages at the edge of the fire.... Breathe in the smell of the cooking food.

Someone hands you a baked potato covered in butter.... What does it taste like?.... You are handed a drink.... Take a drink.... What does it taste like?.... Someone else passes round some toffee.... Try a taste of it.

Now the fire is beginning to die down.... People start to drift off into the dark November night.... You take a last look at the bonfire and turn away to head for home.... How does it feel to say goodbye to the bonfire?.... Go on your way knowing that bonfire night will come again next year.

Now become aware of your breathing again and gently begin to come back to the room.

RUNNING FREE

In this script the students are asked to 'become an animal'. This is an example of how the choice of determining the central image is left to the student. In this way, inferences may be drawn legitimately between the characteristics and behaviour of the animal and the student herself, as long as it is the student who is drawing the inferences.

Take two deep breaths and allow your body to relax.... Just let the tension go.... Imagine that you are somewhere in the open countryside.... Take a good look around.... What does the landscape look like?.... Now in the distance you can just make out something running.... As it moves nearer you can see it is an animal.... What sort of animal is it?.... Just watch it for a while.... How do you feel about the animal?.... Now in imagination try to become the animal.... See what it feels like to be the animal running across the land.... How do you feel about the open space?.... Carry on running.... Just go wherever you want to go.... What are the feelings in your body as you move freely?.... What happens to your breath as you move along?.... Allow your body to do what it wants to do.... Now become yourself again and watch your animal as it runs off into the distance.... Be aware of your feelings as you watch it go.... Now become aware of yourself sitting in your chair and when you feel ready gently come back to the room.

BY THE SEA

This is likely to be an involving fantasy because again it is possible to evoke all the major senses. There may be a proportion of students, though, who have had no first-hand experience of the sea, and this should be checked out first.

> Take two deep breaths and allow your body to relax.... Just let the tension go.... Imagine that you are on the seashore.... It doesn't have to be a place you know or have visited.... Have a good look around you.... What can you see?.... What is the sea like?.... Is it rough or calm?.... Are there any other people around?.... What is the weather like?.... Can you feel the warmth of the sun?.... Can you feel the wind?.... Listen to the sounds of the sea.... What else can you hear?.... What does it smell like by the sea?.... What sort of surface are you sitting or standing on?.... How do you feel being here by the sea?.... Now, in imagination, set off to look for a special shell.... Start to look along the shore, in the sand and in rock pools.... As you look, none of the shells seem quite right – broken or too dull.... What other creatures can you see in the water?.... What is the seaweed like?.... Just along the beach you can see the sun glinting in a pool.... In the pool, you find your special shell.... Pick it up and have a good look at it.... What is its shape?.... What are its colours?.... Feel the texture of the shell.... How do you feel holding the shell?.... Now put your shell somewhere safe and slowly walk back to where you left your things.... Remember, the shell will always be in that safe place if you want to go back and look at it again.... When it is right for you, breathe a little deeper and begin to come back to the room.

Here we have used the device of creating a safe place to put objects of special value that the student can return to at will. This can model an important social and emotional skill for the student in her personal life. It can help create the notion of an inner privacy and an inviolability which, certainly for some students under extreme emotional or physical threat, can be a therapeutic strategy.

A SAFE PLACE

Here we extend the skill of building up a safe psychological space to provide a resource that the student can call on at will. This could be construed as an escape or an avoidance of real-life issues, but we would contend that some measure of inner strength is needed in order to face the vicissitudes of normal living. Having a safe place also enhances the student's ability to rely on her own emotional resources. This can be compared to some forms of meditation which move towards creating a still place at the centre.

> Take two deep breaths and allow your body to relax.... Just let the tension go.... For a moment, I would like you to think about some of the things that are making you anxious at this time in your life.... I am not going to ask you to discuss them with anybody, unless you want to.... You don't need to go into them in great detail, but just be aware that there are some things in your life at the moment that you are not too happy about.
>
> Now build up the sense that there is a safe place you can go to where you don't need to worry about any of these things.... Allow a picture to build up in your imagination of the sort of place you could go to where you would feel safe.... What is this place like?.... Take a good look round.... What sort of things do you have in your safe place?.... What are the colours like?.... What does it smell like?.... What do the things in your safe place feel like?.... Now have the sense that you are actually in your safe place.... What are you doing right now in this safe place?.... How are you feeling?.... Remember that you can stay in this place for as long as you want.... Have the sense that you can come back to this place whenever you need to.... Try to hold on to these feelings as you gently come back to the room.

Students are often eager to share their descriptions of the safe places, but they should not be pressed into revealing their anxieties. Teachers may need to decide for themselves strategies for dealing with extremely sensitive material which may emerge. Problems in relationships, pregnancy, physical or sexual abuse, loneliness, death in families are all anxieties that could be present in a cross-section of students. Certainly some of these issues would be within the remit of most PSE courses designed to meet the needs and concerns of adolescents and the added resource of offering students a safe psychological place might be of enormous benefit.

THE RUCKSACK

This script provides an alternative method for students to take a look at issues that may be worrying them. It enables them to take a long hard look at these anxieties and even decide whether they have any real relevance to the present or merely represent a clinging to habitual patterns of responding to anxiety. It also provides a means of clearing the mind in order to concentrate on the task at hand. We have found it particularly useful at the beginning of a course, to help clear away the anxieties that students bring with them.

Take two deep breaths and allow your body to relax.... Just let the tension go.... Imagine that you are walking through the countryside, carrying a heavy rucksack on your back.... Be aware of the countryside around you, the scenery and the weather.... Most of all be aware of the weight of your rucksack as it presses down on your shoulders.... Build up the feeling that the rucksack contains all the worries and anxieties that are affecting your life at the moment.... Now take the rucksack off, place it on the ground and sit down to rest.... Open the pack up carefully and take out the contents one by one.... Examine each one carefully and then place them on the ground next to you.... Be aware of the feelings that go with the different items that you have taken out of your rucksack.... How do you feel about what you can see?.... Have a good look at them spread out before you.... Now begin to put all of these anxieties back into the pack.... Put them all away carefully and close up the pack tightly.... Now find a safe place to put the rucksack.... Somewhere nearby.... Put it away carefully, but if you need to, you can take it with you.... Now walk on, but have the sense that you can always go back and collect the rucksack if you feel you need to.... How does it feel to leave the pack behind?.... How does your back feel now?.... Has your way of walking changed?.... In imagination now, go wherever you want to.... Be aware of where you want to go and how you are feeling.... Just experience the sensation of being without the rucksack.... See if you can hold on to that feeling as you slowly come back to the room.

THE WALL

This is a useful fantasy for exploring what may seem to be 'sticking points' in life. Once again the notion of finding a way through, or as in this case, over an obstacle can encourage students to think creatively about dealing with their own blocks, whatever they may be.

> Just take two deep breaths and allow your body to relax.... Just let the tension go.... Imagine that you are walking through a dull, cheerless landscape.... There are no people around and little of interest to look at.... Be aware of your feelings as you walk along.... The path that you are walking along leads to a high wall which you can see in the distance.... The wall is so high that you cannot see over it.... As you stand in front of it and realise it is blocking your path, be aware of your feelings about it.... What does the wall look like?.... Go up to it and feel the texture of its surface.... Choose the direction that you are going to take in order to find a way round.... After a while you come across a ladder lying by the wall.... Pick it up and lean it against the wall.... It feels firm and safe.... By climbing up the rungs, you can look over.... What can you see?.... What is happening down there on the other side of the wall?.... What do you feel about it?.... Now if you want to you can climb over and permit the fantasy to go in any way you wish.... Find a way in the fantasy to do what you want to do.... When it is right for you, let that fantasy go and gently come back to the room.

DESIGNING YOUR OWN ROOM

Although designing your own room has long been a favourite stimulus for creative work in several areas of the curriculum, in fantasy form it is particularly successful for several reasons. First, it enables students to let go of the more rational constraints placed upon them by everyday experience. Second, it can highlight who the important people are in their lives at the present time; and third, it can offer the possibility of a private sanctuary.

> Take two deep breaths and allow your body to relax.... Just let the tension go.... In imagination, I want you design a

room for yourself.... The sort of room you would most like to have.... Imagine that you have as much money as you want and you can do anything you like.... Remember that you don't have anyone to please but yourself.... Take the images that come.... What sort of furnishings do you have?.... What are the textures and colours like?.... What special objects do you have in your room?.... Remember that you don't have to let anyone into the room if you don't want to.... But you can show it to someone if you like.... Who might that person be?.... Now say goodbye to your room but remember that you can always come back to it if you want to.... When you are ready, slowly come back to this room.

Drawing is a particularly good way of processing this fantasy and we have found that the quality of drawing produced is usually highly creative and imaginative. Students might also be encouraged to talk about who they allowed into their room and why, or indeed their reasons for keeping people out.

FIRST MEMORIES

Reliving early childhood memories tends to produce a high level of involvement among a group of students. It is as if the students have, to some extent, regressed to the age that has been remembered and there is a relaxed but emotional atmosphere in the room. The following script tends to produce mainly memory imagery, but is an extremely good introduction to the process of looking at internal images.

Take two deep breaths and allow your body to relax.... Just let the tension go.... Go back to the time when you were very small.... What is the first thing you can remember?.... Where are you?.... What can you see?.... Don't watch yourself in the memory, be in the memory.... Are there other people there?.... Who are they and what are they doing?.... How do you feel right now?.... Now try to remember another time, when you were even younger if you can.... Where are you now?.... What can you see?.... Again, try to be in the memory.... Are there other people there?.... What are they doing?.... How do you feel?.... Now let those images fade and gently come back to the present.

EARLY SCHOOL DAYS

Starting school is a very emotional time for both parents and students and even as adults it may be possible to recall early school days. These are often bittersweet memories, bound up with the pain of separation and the new-found pleasures of independence. These feelings are also analogous to the emotional struggles of the adolescent and the fantasy can serve as a key to understanding the confusions that abound during this stage of development.

> Take two deep breaths and allow your body to relax.... Just let the tension go.... Go back to the time when you first went to school.... How far back can you remember?.... What was your first classroom like?.... Can you remember the other children?.... How big did the chairs and tables seem to you then?.... How big did the teacher seem?.... What can you remember doing in that classroom?.... Try to be in the classroom right now.... How does it smell?.... How do you feel about being back in this classroom?.... Now let's go outside.... What was the playground like?.... Be in the playground.... What are you doing?.... How do you feel about the other children playing around you?.... Now recall your journey to school.... In imagination, go on that journey again.... What sort of things are you doing?.... What can you see around you on your journey?.... Who do you meet?.... Just take the memories as they come into your mind's eye and let the feelings come up.... Now let those feelings go and gently come back to the room.

THE BIRTHDAY PARTY

The birthday party is a vivid event for school-age students and in this form provides them with an opportunity to explore their feelings about the significant people in their lives. It also enables them to confront feelings of loss or separation in relation to those significant people. The gifts may be construed as emblems that remain even after the person has gone.

Take two deep breaths and allow your body to relax.... Just let the tension go.... Imagine that it is your birthday.... But this is a very special birthday.... Build up the feeling that you have invited the people who mean most to you in the world.... They can be any age and they are each bringing you a gift.... The table is laid and all the food spread out.... How are you feeling right now?.... The door opens and in come your guests.... Who are they and what do they say to you?.... What do you say to them?.... One by one they give you a gift.... Unwrap each one carefully and see what is inside.... Thank each guest for the gift in any way that feels right for you.... Now put them away safely and let the party continue.... Now let the fantasy go anywhere it wants to as the party goes on.... Build up the feeling that soon the party will end and that your guests will leave.... How do you feel about it?.... Say goodbye to each one in turn now and after the last guest has gone close the door behind them.... How do you feel now that everyone has gone?.... Now gently let those feelings go as you begin to come back to the room.

THE TRAIN ENGINE

We include a section on travel scripts later, but have found that this is a particularly good introductory script. Trains are a potent metaphor in the contemporary consciousness and this fantasy draws on some of that power for its impact.

Take two deep breaths and allow your body to relax.... Just let the tension go.... Imagine a train standing at a station.... What is the engine like?.... What sort of trucks or carriages are attached to the engine?.... What colour is it?.... In imagination, become the engine.... How are you feeling standing at the station?.... In a moment you are going to set off.... How do you feel about pulling the rest of the train behind you?.... You start off slowly.... How does it feel?.... What sort of noises are you making?.... As you set off, you are going up a slope, slowly building up speed.... Feel the weight of the train behind you.... Now the rails begin to level off and you can pick up some speed.... Feel the rush of the air as you begin to move faster.... As the rails begin to slope downhill you start to go even faster and the wind rushes past even faster.... See how fast you can go.... How are you feeling now?.... Just let the fantasy continue as it wants until you finally come to a stop at a station.... How are you feeling now you have stopped?.... Try to stay with these feelings as you begin to come back to the room.

Chapter Five

TRAVEL SCRIPTS

The theme of travel or going on a journey appears to be a powerful metaphor for scripted fantasy. The following scripts have forms of travel as their central theme. Perhaps they represent, in some way, a re-enactment of life's journey or of important episodes during a lifetime. They can be seen as harbingers of change in the sense that at the end of the journey you may be in a psychologically different place or even be a changed person. The journey may therefore symbolically represent an exploration of the self.

MAGIC CARPET RIDE

This is a popular theme for scripted fantasy, tapping in as it does to the appeal of the exotic, even sensuous, associations of the magic carpet. Many students will be familiar with this theme from the stories read to them as young children. The combination of the dark night masking the carpet's journey from public gaze and the potency of the magic carpet itself allows for endless imaginative possibilities. It might be interesting to explore with willing participants the difference between what they chose to do under cover of darkness and in the clear light of day.

> Take two deep breaths and allow your body to relax.... Just let the tension go.... I want you to imagine that you are lying on a magic carpet on the floor in your bedroom.... Take a good look at the carpet.... See the patterns woven into it.... Feel the texture of the carpet as you allow yourself to relax.... Build up the sense that the carpet is going to take off in a moment and that your journey will be a safe one.... As you relax a little deeper, you start to feel lighter and the magic carpet

gently begins to rise up into the air.... Be aware of the sensations in your body as the carpet begins to rise.... The carpet floats up, through the window and gently moves out into the night air.... In a moment, allow yourself to sit up and look at the bright stars in the dark night sky.... Feel the vastness of the universe around you.... As you travel through the night, the sun begins to rise over the horizon and you can see the countryside beneath you.... Look over the edge of the carpet and look at the places you are passing over.... Just allow the carpet to go anywhere it wants.... Now let the magic carpet turn around and find its way back to your house.... See the light of your bedroom window and allow the carpet to float gently down through the window and land on the floor.... How do you feel now that you are back home?.... Say good-bye to the magic carpet and when you are ready, breathe a little deeper and gently come back to the room.

EXPLORING THE ATTIC

Attics are places where things that are not in use any more are stored. This may be because they no longer have any value in the owner's present life or because they themselves, while of no practical use, have feelings or memories attached to them. Some things have been stored away which still have a use but have been temporarily forgotten. Some people never throw things out because they might come in handy one day. Once again, these associations provide a powerful link for recognising our habitual ways of behaving and the feelings that accompany them. Quite often the object that is uncovered is an item from early childhood, for example, a teddy bear, and the long-forgotten object may arouse infantile feelings.

Take two deep breaths and allow your body to relax.... Just let the tension go.... In this fantasy, I am going to invite you to explore the attic of a house.... You may not have an attic in your house but that doesn't matter.... It is a room at the top of the house which is often used for storing things that are not being used any more.... Imagine that you are climbing up some stairs that lead up to an attic.... What does it look like up there?.... How are you feeling right now?.... The door to the attic at the top of the stairs is closed.... You try the handle and find that it is a bit stiff.... You have the sense that there are things that used to belong to you in the attic and you want to go in and have a look at them again.... So take hold of the door handle and give it a good push.... At last you manage to push the door open.... Inside the attic there are heaps of boxes and things under covers.... How do you feel as you look around?.... Begin to sort through the things and see what you can find.... Examine them carefully.... Take a good look at them.... Pick them up and feel them.... How do they smell after all this time?.... Looking around, you see a box which contains something very special that used to belong to you.... What is the box like?.... Open the box and see what is inside.... Take the object out and examine it carefully.... How are you feeling?.... How do you feel about the object?.... If you want to, you can take the object with you.... Or put it back where it came from, it's up to you.... Go back to the door and down the stairs again.... Now breathe a little more deeply and when you are ready, gently come back to the room.

We have seen a similar script which involves the exploration of the basement of a house. This is another potent theme, but one which in our experience tends to have a depressing effect on a group, possibly because of the notion of descending into subterranean depths.

EXPLORING A RIVER

This script may be more appropriate for use with older students or at least those who have some appreciation of the physical geography involved. There is no reason why this script should not be used as an adjunct to a geography lesson concerned with the concept of rivers flowing from their source to the sea. Psychologically, the association with the journey of the river from its source to the sea may parallel the changing feelings from infancy to maturity. The waterfall is a rich source of emotional data for participants. Feelings of strength and vitality, power and freedom for some may be contrasted with the experience of being submerged, controlled or taken over by others. In the same way, it is interesting to share the experience of merging with the sea which may throw up similarly contradictory sets of feelings within a group.

Take two deep breaths and allow your body to relax.... Just let the tension go.... Imagine now that you are standing in some hills or mountains.... A place where a river begins.... It doesn't have to be a place you knc w.... Just go along with images that come up.... Where does the river start?.... Take a good look around you.... What is the scenery like?.... How do you feel about being here?.... Are there any other people about?.... Again, take a good look at the source of the river.... Become aware of the water.... How clear it is.... The way that it flows.... Dip your hand in the water and be aware of how it feels, its temperature.... Take some of the water up into your hands and taste it.... Be aware of the sound of the water as it flows along.... Now start to explore the river by walking along the bank.... Be aware of how it changes as you walk along and how the scenery changes.... As you continue your journey, build up the feeling that round the next bend you are going to come to a waterfall.... Turn the bend and see what the waterfall is like.... How high it is and the amount of water that flows over the edge.... Now, in imagination, if it is comfortable for you, try to become the water in the stream.... What does this feel like?.... In imagination, go with the flow of the stream as it quickens and flows over the waterfall.... For a moment hold the feeling of the water flowing over the fall.... Feel it as a bodily sensation.... Now return to yourself exploring the river and continue on your journey as other streams join and increase the amount of water.... Be aware of how much water there is now and what that water is like.... What sort of countryside are you travelling through?.... How do you feel now as you walk along?.... Now you come to the place where the river meets the sea.... What is the scenery like here?.... What are you doing now?.... How do you feel?.... If it is comfortable for you, become the water in the river again as it merges into the sea.... Be aware of how this feels.... Now breathe a little more deeply and when it is right for you, gently come back to the room.

EXPLORING THE BODY

This script involves inviting students to 'become' significant elements in the fantasy and then to generate a dialogue between the elements and themselves. Adding a new dimension of communication between elements makes this script more appropriate to use with a group which has had some previous experience of scripted fantasy work. This is not to say that generating a dialogue between elements in a fantasy is a difficult undertaking, but that the unfamiliarity of the activity may block the responses of some students.

Although there seems to be a fairly overt mind/body, cognitive/affective split contained within the fantasy via the brain and heart elements, it would be a mistake to presume that the students' construction of these elements is as clear cut as the dichotomy would suggest. What often emerges is that brains have feelings, too.

Take two deep breaths and allow your body to relax.... Just let the tension go.... Now I want you to image that you are becoming very small, so small that you could go into your own mouth and explore your body.... First make sure you have shrunk to the right size and have the sense that you have become very small.... What is it like being so small?.... Now imagine that you are standing on the edge of your lips and find a way of going down into your body.... You don't need to worry about what the body is really like, just go along with the images that come.... What can you see?.... How do you feel about being here?.... Just go along in any way you want and see where you go.... How easy is it for you to travel around?.... Now in imagination see if you can find a way to get to your brain.... What is your brain like?.... What is happening there?.... In imagination try to become the brain and see what that is like.... How does it feel being the brain?.... What is your life as the brain like?.... What do think of that tiny person who is looking at you?.... Now see if you have anything you would like to say to the tiny person.... In imagination, just say anything that comes.... Now become yourself again and talk back to the brain.... Let the discussion go on as it likes.... Now let that conversation go.... As the tiny person, continue your journey through the body.... What can you see next?.... What sounds can you hear as you travel along?....

Just go along with the pictures that come.... In imagination find a way to your heart.... When you find it, take a good look at it.... What does it look like?.... What is it doing?.... Now try to become the heart.... See what it feels like to be the heart.... What do you think of the tiny person who is looking at you?.... In imagination, see if you have anything to say to the tiny person.... Anything that comes into your mind.... Now become yourself and talk back to the heart.... Say anything that comes.... Let the discussion go on as it likes.... Now become the tiny person again and see how you are feeling right now.... How do you feel about the things that the heart and the body have been saying to you?.... Now slowly allow yourself to expand, and as you grow, start to merge with your larger real body.... Until the tiny person and your real body become the same.... Breathe a little deeper and now when you are ready gently come back to the room.

CLIMBING A MOUNTAIN

Like the journey of a river from its source to the sea, climbing a mountain is an extended fantasy for older, more practised students who are familiar with the technique of a dialogue between the elements. It may be that the teacher would want to highlight the dialogue during the processing of the fantasy and this is suitable as both a listening and writing exercise. Even brainstorming the feelings associated with each of the elements, mountain, wind and self, in fantasy can prove a rich source of personal data. Students may begin to look at apparently contradictory sets of emotions and learn to accept that there are many different facets of the self. Readers may recognise Gestalt theory in this approach to the self and we will return to this theme in a later chapter.

Take two deep breaths and allow your body to relax.... Just let the tension go.... I want you to imagine that you are sitting on a fence admiring a mountain in the distance.... Your intention is to journey to the top of the mountain and you have all that you need with you.... How are you dressed?.... What equipment have you got?.... Take a good look at the mountain and become aware of its shape, its colours, the vegetation growing around it.... How do you feel about this jour-

ney you are about to undertake?.... Now set off on your journey and just allow yourself to go along with the images that
come.... As you follow the path up the mountain, become
aware of your feelings.... Be aware of the changing scenery....
What is the weather like?.... Is it warm or cool?.... What does
the air smell like?.... How steep is your path?.... Can you just
walk, or do you have to scramble or climb?.... Carry on your
journey and be aware of what is happening and how you are
feeling.... Now take a rest and have a good look at the view....
How far have you come up the mountain?.... In imagination,
become the mountain and see what that feels like.... What is
your life like as the mountain?.... What do you think of this
person who is climbing you?.... See if you have some advice to
give to the person who is climbing you.... Try answering in
imagination.... Now become yourself again and see how you
ʳ ᵉl about what the mountain has said.... Try saying some-
tı. ɪg back to the mountain.... Anything that comes.... Now
cor.ɪnue on your journey but be aware of how you are feeling aɴd how difficult it is.... Continue until finally you reach
the top ᴏf the mountain.... If you haven't managed to get to
the top, juᵌᵗ imagine that you are there.... How does it feel to
be at the top of the mountain?.... What can you see?.... Have
a good look around.... Now become aware of the wind or
breeze at the top of the mountain.... Be aware of how it feels
against your face and what temperature it is.... Now, in imagination, become the wind.... How do you feel as the
wind?.... What is your life like as the wind?.... What do you
think of this person standing at the top of the mountain?....
See if you have something to say to this person.... Try saying
it.... Anything that comes.... Now become yourself again and
see what you feel about what the wind said to you.... Reply to
the wind.... Imagine a conversation between the two of you....
Now imagine that you have found a way down the mountain
and you are walking home in the evening sun.... For a moment, look back at the mountain and be aware of how you
are feeling.... Then carry on with your journey home.... Now
breathe a little more deeply and when you are ready, gently
begin to come back to the room.

THE HOT AIR BALLOON

The grace and elegance of a hot air balloon in flight readily appeals to the imagination. A journey in a hot air balloon provides the traveller with an opportunity to look at the world from a different perspective and psychologically the fantasy journey may offer students the same possibility. Flight need not necessarily be construed with the somewhat negative connotation of escape. The flight of the balloon enables the traveller to broaden her horizons quite literally, to see possibilities where they did not exist before. Making the decision to jump into the balloon is rather like a leap of faith, that once we decide to take the risk of change we may never see things in the same way again. This particular fantasy may be useful for a group of students who have come to a point in their lives at which they need to make a decision or a change, for example, choosing subject options, leaving school, or going to college and so on.

Take two deep breaths and allow your body to relax.... Just let the tension go.... I want you to imagine that you are in a park where you can see a group of people blowing up a hot air balloon ready for a trip.... There is a large basket with gas burners on the top and the balloon is stretched out on the ground.... You watch the balloon slowly fill with hot air.... Someone calls you over and asks you to hold a rope while the balloon is filling up.... Just as the basket is about to set off, you are asked if you want to go for a ride.... Make a quick decision and allow yourself to jump up into the basket; you know the trip will be a safe one.... The ropes are let go and the balloon sets off.... The crowd gives a cheer as the balloon rises high above the trees.... How do you feel as you begin to soar up into the air?.... What is the weather like?.... Feel the wind against your face and in your hair.... Now you find the balloon is passing over the place where you live.... What is happening down there?.... You can see people you know.... Who are they and what are they doing?.... What do you think about what is happening down there?.... Now the balloon begins to drift away.... After a while it floats over a part of the countryside which is very different from the place where you live.... What does it look like?.... Are there any people about?.... What do you think about what is going on down there?.... Now the wind changes and the balloon soars high up into the sky.... Just go along with the images of where you go and what you can see.... Now the balloon slowly drifts back to the park from where you began your journey and gently lands on the grass.... As the balloon slowly deflates, breathe a little more deeply and gently begin to come back to the room.

THE TIME MACHINE

Traditionally, the time machine has been used by science fiction writers as a device for taking 'man' beyond the confines of the present into realms of time and space unfettered by the limitations of normal experience and the need for the rationality of sequential time. Despite the fact that the time machine has been captured in the popular imagination by the TV series 'Dr Who', there is still room for students to expand their powers of imagination beyond the TV screen.

Contained within the fantasy are fairly advanced notions of time and space which would make it unsuitable for students who have not yet grasped these concepts.

From our own experience of programmes like 'Dr Who' and other works of science fiction, there is always a possibility of strange alien creatures appearing or of being stranded in a different time dimension. With this in mind we have incorporated two suggestions: that this particular time machine is completely under the control of the student ('You can come back any time you want') and that the journey will be a safe one. This does not preclude the possibility of unpleasant things happening but does provide the security of escape.

Take two deep breaths and allow your body to relax.... Just let the tension go.... I want you to imagine that you are in your bedroom at home.... The curtains are shut.... Begin to build up a feeling that when you open them you will see something extraordinary outside.... Now open the curtains and there outside you see a time machine.... Take a good look at it.... What does it look like?.... What do you feel about the time machine?.... Build up the sense that you are going to travel through time.... If you decide to, you know it will be a safe journey and that you can come back any time you want.... Make your way downstairs and out through the front door.... Now find a way into the time machine.... What does it look like inside?.... How are you feeling right now?.... Find the controls which start the time machine.... Switch the engine on.... Now allow the time machine to travel off through time and space.... Just permit it to go where it wants to.... How are you feeling now?.... Build up the feeling that the time machine is about to land.... Let it land.... How does it feel to have landed?.... Decide whether you want to go outside and explore this new place or stay inside and just look out through the window.... It doesn't matter which you decide to do.... Take a good look around.... What do you see?.... What is the landscape like?.... What is the vegetation like?.... Are there any buildings?.... Can you see any animal life?.... Are there any people about?.... If there are, how are they dressed?.... Try to guess what period of time you have travelled to.... Now find a person to talk to.... Do they speak the same language as you do?.... Ask the person what it is like to live in this time and this place.... How do they reply?.... Tell the person what it's like living in your time and place.... Now allow the fantasy to go anywhere it wants to for a while.... Build up the feeling that soon you will have to return to the time machine.... Find a way of thanking the person you had been talking to and say goodbye.... Make your way back to the time machine and set the controls to take you back home, into the here and now.... How do you feel as you set off for home and leave this place behind?.... Soon the time machine will land.... Permit it to land right now.... Leave the time machine and say goodbye.... How do you feel being back home and seeing the time machine disappear?.... Remember that in imagination you can recall your time machine any time you want to.... Now breathe a little more deeply and when you are ready, gently begin to come back to the room.

Chapter Six

OUTCOMES OF USING SCRIPTED FANTASY IN THE CLASSROOM

The material under discussion in this section is based on reports from many teachers over a number of years. These teachers have been trained and received supervision in the use of these techniques on Human Relations courses at the School of Education, Nottingham University. The reports come from teachers working in a wide range of educational institutions, including schools for maladjusted students, sixth-form colleges, infant schools and further education colleges – in effect, all parts of the education system.

PREDICTIONS AND OUTCOMES

It is important that the teacher be aware of the possible effects of a particular script. With this in mind we have provided a brief introduction to each of the scripts. We have pointed out, for example, that a script involving an extended downward movement, such as going down into a basement or deep into a cave, might induce feelings of depression in some students. You may wish to avoid this or you may not. Whatever decision you make professionally, we would argue, needs to be founded upon a dual level of awareness within the teacher herself.

One level of awareness concerns the cognitive recognition of the outcomes resulting from specific factors contained within the structure of the fantasy itself. To return to the example of the basement, the teacher understands that the possibility of depression exists as an outcome of this particular fantasy and makes a judgement about its suitability based on the context of the course in which it is to be used, the timing of the intervention and the specific perceived needs of the student group.

The second level of awareness, which may unwittingly interfere with the first, is that a teacher who is unable to face feelings of depression in her own life will generalize that response outwards onto the students and conclude, perhaps mistakenly, that they cannot cope with such feelings either.

In this way the teacher is in danger of imposing her personal expectations on what she feels the outcomes of using fantasy are likely to be. What we have been at pains to emphasise is that a specific script will produce a range of different feelings and it is crucial that the teacher does not manipulate the script or the students into producing the feelings she thinks are desirable. Using the example of the basement once more, having decided to use it with a group the teacher might try to gloss over any feelings of depression that may emerge or be articulated and pretend either that they don't exist or that everything will 'be all right'. The denial of the teacher's own depression can result in the denial of feelings of depression in the group.

It is the responsibility of the teacher who wishes to use scripted fantasy in the classroon to monitor constantly the interface between the cognitive and affective levels of awareness, in order to prevent the working out of personal issues, concerns and agendas through the students. The same mistake can be made in helping students to understand 'moral' behaviour. The teacher by definition is a powerful person in the classroom. Using fantasy adds to this power. Teachers should be conscious of the responsibility that this power carries with it and use it with awareness.

In spite of our aversion for prediction, there are certain kinds of behaviour and responses that tend to occur consistently during and following a fantasy experience. For a number of years we have asked teachers to keep a record of the experiential fantasy work they do in schools. Several broad themes recur throughout these reports.

Resistance

There were many reports of resistance to the activity from students, especially those of secondary school age. The resistance expressed itself in various forms such as giggling, moving around and complaints that 'this is stupid' or 'it's not proper work'. The reason behind the resistance will be different for each individual, but we would guess that it is commonly bound up with the risk of revealing aspects of the self that are normally untouched by the conventional educational process. Schools are very much places of predictability and routine and it is as if something that is not properly understood or is out of the ordinary has to be dismissed. Teachers and students share a strong preconception of what is acceptable during a school day; this does not include being relaxed and having fantasies. If, as the teacher, you break out of the conventional patterns that the school sets, then the students may be unable to respond with their well-learned, well-practised games. The students who complain that 'this isn't proper work' may often be those who refuse to do the 'proper' work anyway.

Students who have been successful academically in school also demonstrate some initial resistance to the technique. Many complain that such work won't get them their GCSEs. For students whose sense of self-esteem is linked so closely to academic success and the emotional pay-off that it brings, this form of defence mechanism is understandable. Some also construe themselves to be at the top of an academic pecking order and are unhappy at engaging in activities that are not marked, assessed or judged in the conventional manner. Students like this need to be given a careful rationale for the activity, perhaps one in terms of developing all aspects of their being, emotional as well as intellectual.

This behaviour is not confined to school-age students. We have witnessed many of the same manifestations of resistance among teachers on in-service courses. Sometimes the word 'fantasy' produces guilty sniggers from both older students and teachers, implying that fantasy is bound to have sexual connotations. This may be because of a confusion of terms with daydreaming, which for some may be predominantly sexual in content.

Back in the classroom, the teacher has the choice of stopping the activity or understanding and accepting what may lie behind the resistance and continuing as planned. It is surprising how much disturbance can go on without preventing the majority of students from becoming involved with the fantasy. This is particularly true of infant classes, where young students often provide a running commentary as the fantasy images emerge. In our experience, the student who appears to have been the most disruptive is still able to report back in a way that shows that she has been involved. Try paying attention to some of the genuine anxieties that are being voiced, while not allowing yourself to be seduced into abandoning your programme. If students are being asked to risk trying out a different activity, then some reassurance may be necessary, but reassurance need not mean colluding to reinforce that resistance.

If the level of resistance being expressed becomes too disruptive then it may be necessary to stop. The problem could be put to the group and it is at this point that it may be appropriate to offer the choice of joining in or opting out. You could suggest that the real objectors either find something to do quietly or, if it is appropriate, leave the room. It is important to remember that this strategy is not a discipline measure, but rather an attempt to work out an amicable solution to the presenting problem. Sometimes their peers will put pressure on them to be quiet. By giving the students a choice they often become more responsible for making the lesson work. This may result in their being willing to continue with the fantasy. However, you may decide that what you planned to do was not suitable for that particular class at that particular time. You could then try something different. It is important not to see this as a failure either for yourself or for the students. Some preparatory work may need to be done to help the class build up their confidence so that they are prepared to try out new activities. Or it may be that there is insufficient trust amongst the group. In this case, you will have to work hard to improve the prevailing climate of trust.

Involvement

In spite of the resistance described in the preceding section, most participants will have an involving fantasy experience. Even students who refuse to close their eyes seem to be able to project an image in front of them. The same is true for teachers who, paradoxically, report that they have not had a fantasy at all and then go on to discuss the fantasy that they have not had in great detail. It is as though people have a very fixed idea about what a fantasy ought to be, which they cling to even in the face of contradictory evidence from their own experience.

A small minority of students and teachers still claim to experience no imagery at all, while others report feeling rather unsettled by the fantasy. This is not necessarily a bad thing, as one point of view is that learning can only come out of discomfort and confusion (Joyce, 1984). Touching on important issues in a person's life may be disturbing, as considerable effort is often expended avoiding them. Further evidence that there has been a high level of involvement comes with the invariable request for more fantasy work, both from students in school and teachers on in-service courses.

In spite of this resistance, we would suggest that fantasy can provide an opportunity for a group to be involved in a co-operative, relaxing activity, exploring aspects of their feelings and behaviour that are not normally attended to in the course of a school day. Working through an initial resistance to the activity may bring these not inconsiderable gains.

Relaxation

The most vivid examples of the relaxing effects of scripted fantasy come from the reports of teachers of emotionally disturbed children. Quite independently, two teachers reported their experiences with student groups. Both teachers felt unsettled and anxious because of the high level of disruption that went on as the fantasy script was being read out. Despite their doubts about the wisdom of persevering, they continued until they had finished the script. What surprised them most of all was the ensuing discussions. They said that virtually all of the students joined in and, atypically, were involved and co-operative.

Both teachers reported that the classes were relaxed and subdued for the rest of the day, which is extremely unusual for students with behavioural difficulties. The learning here seems to be about not having unrealistic expectations about the behaviour of student groups during the activity. If, from your previous experience of a group, they appear to be boisterous, assertive or questioning, then they are unlikely to be quiet just because you have suggested that they relax in preparation for a fantasy. Only by participating in the experience will students become familiar with the benefits that accrue from following the teacher's instructions.

These relaxing effects were also noted by the experience of a science teacher who used a scripted fantasy with a group of fifteen-year-olds to try to facilitate insight into the movements of subatomic particles. In previous lessons the class invariably indulged in some form of disruptive behaviour and were difficult to control. The fantasy was conducted sitting on stools at laboratory benches, not the ideal situation for work of this nature. Nevertheless, the teacher described how the students spent the rest of the lesson working

quietly or talking in hushed tones, an atmosphere he had not previously experienced with that class.

On a larger scale, this induction of relaxation as a result of using
a fantasy script was reported by the teacher who introduced a short
fantasy into morning assembly in a large comprehensive school.
He used an abridged version of the 'Wise Man Fantasy' taken from
John Stevens's (1971) book *Awareness,* and then asked the students
to turn to a neighbour and talk about their experience. He reported
a high degree of involvement in the discussion, which was conducted in quiet tones. He found that they were unusually reluctant
to leave assembly and go to the first lesson of the day. Later, six
teachers commented on the relaxed and positive attitudes of their
students during the first lesson (Williams, 1985).

These three examples provide reassurance for the apprehension
involved in the common statement, 'I couldn't possibly do fantasy
work like this with my students; they would never co-operate'. One
of the writers had a class who would co-operate in little except fantasy work and this work appeared to improve relationships over
time.

A more therapeutic application of fantasy is reported by the
teacher who was asked to try to help with a student who was having
hysterics because of a bout of homesickness during a school trip
abroad. She gently led the student through a fantasy journey of
being by the seashore and he soon fell asleep. The student appeared
to be happy for the rest of the trip and, as a result of her intervention, the teacher was perceived by her colleagues as having mysterious powers!

Discussion and art work

An important outcome from the use of scripted fantasy is the improved quality of discussion that follows the experience. This was
reported almost universally by more than 200 teachers. They
claimed that discussion focused on processing a fantasy produced
a high level of motivation and energy among the students. They
also commented that students who rarely spoke in front of the
whole group made contributions and that there was a noticeable
improvement in the quality and length of the discussion itself. Most
experienced teachers would describe this as a considerable gain.

The point is often made that fantasy generates what is described as a whole group discussion. When one person is talking, everyone else is listening, interested and supportive. This may be partly attributable to the fact that although each student has a unique contribution to make, there is no inherent source of conflict, competition or argument contained within the material. It is one of the few times in a classroom that differences are accepted without dissent. The teacher and the more powerful, assertive members of the class tend not to dominate the discussion. Autonomy is encouraged as students learn to value their own contributions and are less inclined to allow the more voluble members of the group to dominate the talking.

This same sense of independence and self-assurance is to be found in their art work. At times during the course of a conventional art class, the student who feels insecure about her abilities will quite unconsciously copy the ideas of a neighbour. This never seems to happen in the art work produced following a fantasy. It is as if the fear of being judged and the self-imposed restraints on the imagination have been let go. Further evidence of this liberating effect is seen in the quality of the art work produced. Although reports of this phenomenon are subjective, accounts of improvement are so universal as to make them highly credible, even allowing for the added motivation of a novel activity.

Teachers reported that students seemed to take pleasure from the work they produced following a fantasy. Those teachers who took the trouble to display students' work commented that the students appeared to be fascinated not only by their own work but also by the rest of the group's. The scrutiny of the work often took place in total silence. Teachers who have experienced this phenomenon report that they have been extremely impressed, even moved by the atmosphere generated by the activity. Self-imposed silence by students is a rare occurrence in schools.

Memorability

Some people find that they can recall significant details of their scripted fantasies years later. We have had the experience of meeting past students who have commented, 'I'll never forget the time you did the fantasy of ... with us', while details of other more conventional lessons have long since faded. The degree of personal involvement and vividness of the internal imagery produces a highly memorable experience.

This quality that fantasy and imagery have of being highly memorable can serve a useful function in the classroom. Two biology teachers reported that any technical terms introduced during a scripted fantasy were retained better than when they were introduced in the course of normal instruction. The two fantasies employed by the teachers involved respectively, a butterfly landing on a leaf and a seed of corn growing. The appropriate technical terms were woven into the script. No attempt was made to gather this data rigorously, but it is in line with the findings of memorability and imagery going back to Bartlett (1932). He showed that images are remembered better than words. Images can be used to remember complex lists of terms and there is no doubt that certain subject areas call for the retention of vast amounts of information. There is no reason why fantasy cannot be harnessed creatively to help with this process.

There is a difference between using fantasy for its own sake and as a memory aid. Certainly, as a memory aid, the success of the technique may lie in the receptivity of the group due to their relaxed state. In contrast, references by students to past fantasy experiences seem to indicate the personal significance of the experience for the students.

An example of this was experienced by one of the writers using fantasy with a group of twelve-year-olds in an inner-city comprehensive school. The students were invited to take part in a fantasy journey and were given the choice to opt out if they wished. One of the girls, Christina, stated that this was a stupid thing to do and sat through the exercise with her arms folded, staring up at the ceiling with a defiant expression on her face. Part of the fantasy involved writing your name over and over again to cover two sheets of blank paper. Three months later, Christina's mother came to the school for a parents' evening and reported that her daughter had done a strange thing some time ago. She had taken a large sheet of paper, written her name all over it, thrown it into the fire and said, 'Thank goodness that's done!' It is difficult to know what conclusions to draw from this, but it does suggest that despite her denial, the session was a vivid experience for Christina and the after-effects were memorable even for her mother.

Co-operation

Another very positive aspect of using fantasy in the classroom is that it tends to promote a co-operative working atmosphere. An example of this was provided by a teacher of rural science. He asked his class to go through a fantasy that involved designing their 'perfect room'. At the end of the fantasy he invited the students to tidy up their perfect rooms. Curiously, at the end of the afternoon, the same class spontaneously cleaned all the tools and tidied them away. Normally the teacher had to bully and cajole the class to do this and he felt that this increase in co-operative behaviour was directly attributable to the fantasy experience.

Joanne was a member of a class of fourteen-year-olds who were involved in some extended research by two of the writers into scripted fantasy. This involved a complex procedure in which students rated elements in their fantasy experience using repertory grids (Hall, 1983). She later asked for a copy of all the instructions and went through the same procedures with her mother and younger brother, a process involving several hours' work. She brought in a full set of viable data for analysis. This degree of involvement seems atypical of adolescents and indicates the depth of identification with the task. Both Joanne and the rest of the group displayed a high degree of co-operation in completing a complex task.

One teacher reported that as her class came into the room, she noticed that one girl was visibly upset and that a small group of students was tense and agitated. On the spur of the moment she decided to lead the class in a short relaxation and a script in which the students imagined a storm on a lake, which slowly subsided until the wind had died down and the lake was still and calm. In discussion, the girl who had been in tears was able to talk about the upsetting incident in a calm, matter-of-fact way. With all the emotional disturbance behind them, the class worked both co-operatively and in an involved manner, which the teacher attributed directly to the calming influence of the fantasy.

QUALITY OF WRITING AND THE EXPRESSION OF FEELING

Many teachers have asked their students to write about their fantasy journeys. A frequent statement about this writing is that it is of a better quality, is better presented and includes a more frequent and more subtle use of statements of feeling. This is not surprising if, as we have reported, the fantasy journeys are both memorable and emotional experiences.

Aspects of fantasy have always been used by the creative English teacher as a stimulus for writing and this approach is now being extended to other subject areas like PSE. With the development of humanistic techniques in education, increasing numbers of teachers use scripted fantasy and employ writing as a means of processing the experience.

An evaluation of these written responses has been undertaken by one of the writers (Hall and Kirkland, 1984; and Hall and Greenwood, 1986). These two studies support our claim that a fantasy stimulus tends to produce writing that is of higher quality and is better presented, and includes a higher proportion of statements of feeling.

These studies involved classes of young adolescents in comprehensive schools. They were asked to draw a tree and were then taken through a short fantasy of what it was like to be the tree they had drawn. Finally, they were asked to write about the fantasy and encouraged to use the first-person 'I', as if they were the tree in their fantasy.

It is difficult to decide precisely what constitutes a statement of feeling, but using a simple counting procedure, involving two independent raters, more than double the number of statements of feeling were found in the writing stimulated by fantasy.

The quality of the writing was much more difficult to assess. The teachers who conducted the lessons were perceived to be outstanding at their craft by their colleagues and enjoyed teaching the art of creative writing. After trying out the fantasy procedures, the teachers reported that the previous writing their students had produced was comparatively flat and full of cliché, that narratives did not concentrate on single events and particular situations and emotions tended to be generalized. Words and phrases like, 'happy', 'frightened', 'awful', 'I feel strongly', 'it was sad', were used repeatedly and the writing lacked individual and personal detail. Where there had been an initial discussion of the topic, students often regurgitated the phrases used in the discussion. There was little evidence of searching for the most accurate or evocative word or image.

This assessment was in stark contrast to the responses to the tree fantasy, which produced particularly vivid themes, many of which had to do with misery, mutilation or death.

> In winter no one wants to know me, I shiver to my roots, they are going to dig me up.

> Soon I shall be no more because they are building a new estate.... People say it's as if I am waving my branches for help.... I will just be burnt with all the other rubbish.... I am a rotten old tree.

They wrote of their longing for youth again and regretted their age and 'shrivelled roots'. Death was a recurrent theme, including the anticipation of their own deaths. One account demonstrated a poignant merging of fantasy and reality.

> My Grandad had to go away to the wood for a couple of weeks and he got chopped down for firewood. We got a telegram five days ago, she was sad and still is a little now but she will be OK she's nice my Gran so I like her staying with us.

Below is a complete example:

> I am the tree and I am jealous. Jealous of all the trees around me who are full of life, for I am dying. They tried to save me by cutting off an infected branch. Some of my bark is split off and ivy is crawling around me. Fungus is sprouting out everywhere. I have very little feeling in my roots which are cold all the year round. A family of birds used to nest in my branches, but they soon found a better tree, they didn't want to live in manky rotten tree. I wish someone would chop me down and not keep me suffering until death. I wish I would die right now so that the pain and sadness will not worry me any longer.

This is an extremely melancholy account but it is typical of the work produced. It would seem that the tree drawing and subsequent fantasy produced an outpouring of feelings that might be perceived as negative. We would not want to subscribe to the notion that powerful writing about pain, suffering or death should be construed as negative. We would argue that they represent one end of a continuum of human feelings and emotions so that denial of difficult feelings is both futile and damaging.

If we accept that these students were projecting their own thoughts and feelings into the fantasy experience and writing, then they would appear to be harbouring a great deal of anxiety, sadness, hurt and anger. Young adolescents, however, sometimes resist the suggestion that they have said anything important about themselves through their writing and it would probably require the intervention of a skilful counsellor to facilitate this sort of connection. However, some students unconsciously acknowledge the link with statements such as:

Writing out everything cheers me up.

In English you can unfold and let the teachers know what you feel.

Young adolescents are not reticent about expressing their feelings but the feelings are often directed outward and usually related to likes and dislikes. The feelings that emerged repeatedly in the writing generated by some of the fantasies – anxiety, sadness, hurt and anger – are probably actively discouraged by the adolescent peer-group and indeed by our culture. When anger is expressed by young adolescents, it tends to be acted out in a distorted, sometimes anti-social form.

It is important to ask what is the point of all this outpouring of feelings. Certainly from the English teacher's point of view, the accurate expression of a sophisticated range of feeling in written form is a common goal. From the point of view of teachers involved in PSHE (Personal, Social and Health Education) there does seem to be considerable indirect evidence (Simonton, Matthews-Simonton and Creighton, 1980) that the expression of feeling can help to offset subsequent psychosomatic disturbances. Exercises of this nature could be providing an important psychological safety valve for the students concerned. All of the teachers reported being shocked by the proportion of so-called negative feelings produced by groups of young adolescents from a wide variety of backgrounds.

At the same time the teachers were convinced of the authenticity of the statements and felt that they knew and understood the students better as a result of reading their work.

A possible explanation for the increase in statements of feeling following the fantasy procedures is that fantasy produces an immediate experience of feeling, vestiges of which are still present during the writing. In this way the writing becomes a direct expression of felt emotion, whereas normal creative writing involves the vicarious description of feelings. This difference between self-expression and description may explain the lack of vitality and energy in much creative writing produced in schools.

SUMMARY

The period following a scripted fantasy involves an increase in behaviour that teachers consider desirable. The students are more relaxed and quiet. Their written and art work based on the fantasies are reported to be of a markedly improved quality. Students who normally say very little join in group discussions and speak in longer sentences. There are also reports that these gains extend into the lessons that follow and appear to produce a noticeable improvement in the quality of the learning experience. Singer (1973) in his book, *The Child's World of Make-Believe*, provides statistical evidence to show that encouraging imagination and creativity enhances students' ability to cope and learn.

There are not many occasions when a whole class is listening to the teacher and following her suggestions. At the same time the students can do exactly what they want within the bounds of the fantasy. The class is involved in a co-operative activity while simultaneously undergoing a very private and individual experience.

The outcomes we have reported may seem the stuff that many stressed and harassed teachers might dream of, yet with preparation, trust and a willingness to develop new skills, undertaking this activity it is within the grasp of all.

Chapter Seven

GROWTH SCRIPTS

The school-age years, between five and eighteen, are a period of rapid, accelerated, physical and emotional development. For many students this is a period in which the constraints of the socialising process can produce confusion, frustration and guilt. In addition, the hormonal surges that characterise the onset of puberty produce an emotional see-sawing between highs and lows which can create problematic situations in classrooms. Although teachers are aware of and understand these issues at an intellectual level, many find it hard to address the question of how to facilitate students' appropriate expression of feelings in the classroom.

Using scripted fantasy gives students an effective means of tuning into the processes that are taking place in their bodies and minds. It can provide them with a legitimate opportunity to conceptualise and verbalise thoughts and feelings about growing up and share their experiences with each other. Scripts that have growth as a central theme can be used most effectively in this context. Images of growth can be seen as metaphors for change or even for reviewing rites of passage in life, and can serve as a potent stimulus to explore feelings that are often poorly understood. In this way, students are enabled to review their behaviour and perhaps determine ways they might develop their potential more effectively. The following scripts form a basis for the creative exploration of these notions of growth and development.

THE CHRYSALIS

'The Chrysalis' is a script that could fit happily into a science or PSE lesson, depending upon the aims and objectives of the teacher. In either case it gives students the opportunity to explore the feelings involved with breaking out of existing limits. It could also be used as an effective stimulus for dance or movement with younger students of primary age.

> Take two deep breaths and allow your body to relax.... Just let the tension go.... Imagine that you are a chrysalis.... Don't see yourself as a chrysalis, actually be the chrysalis inside your case.... Be aware of the position you are in.... Of how your limbs are folded.... How do you fit inside your case?.... Is it a tight or a loose fit?.... Be aware of the texture of the case.... How does it feel?.... Is it hard or soft?.... What is it like?.... Feel the texture against you.... How do you feel being this chrysalis, inside this case?.... Now feel the sun shining on the outside of your case.... It is getting warmer.... Build up the feeling that the time has come for a change, that your body needs to expand.... You are aware that in a while you will be able to emerge from your chrysalis.... Feel the pressure of your case again.... Now as the sun becomes warmer, be aware of the point at which the the case begins to give way.... Feel the case opening.... See if you can move your body.... Take your time and be aware of how you are feeling as you emerge from the case.... What is happening to your body?.... What do you look like now you have emerged from your chrysalis?.... How are you feeling?.... What are you doing?.... When it is right for you, breathe a little more deeply, open your eyes and have a look at the other people in the room.

With a carpeted room it is possible to encourage students to try out this fantasy curled up in a foetal position. They can be invited to make the movements that go with breaking out of the chrysalis as the fantasy progresses.

THE SEED

Like 'The Chrysalis', 'The Seed' has cross-curricular applications. For teachers of biology or rural science the script could be modified to fit the input of a particular lesson, so that the seed is named and the physical description prescribed. Nevertheless, it would be inappropriate to concentrate solely on the cognitive aspects of the learning and students should be allowed to talk about the feelings that emerged during the fantasy.

> Take two deep breaths and allow your body to relax.... Just let the tension go.... I want you to imagine that you are a seed in the ground.... What size are you?.... Be aware of what it feels like to be in the ground.... What does the soil feel like?.... Is it damp or dry?.... Is it warm or cold?.... Is it hard or soft?.... Now build up the sense that the ground is becoming warmer.... That some refreshing rain is seeping down through the soil.... How does that feel?.... With the warmth and the moisture you feel yourself start to expand.... Roots begin to extend down into the ground.... You begin to open out at the top and a stem begins to grow up to the surface of the ground.... As you grow into a seedling you break through to the surface.... What does it feel like as you break through the ground and come out into the light and the open air?.... What sort of plant are you growing into?.... What is your stem like?.... What are your leaves like?.... Do you have flowers?.... Allow the growth to continue until you become a fully grown plant.... What does it feel like to be a fully grown plant?.... Take a good look at yourself.... What do you look like?.... What do you feel about yourself now?.... Take a good look around.... Is there anything growing nearby?.... How do you feel about what you see?.... When you are ready find a way of saying goodbye to your plant.... Now breathe a little more deeply and gently begin to come back to the room.

This fantasy can be extended by taking the mature plant through the seasonal changes. This could be done either by looking at the full cycle of seasons and exploring feelings about the changes or taking a single season and allowing students to explore their feelings in more depth.

THE ROSE

Enhancing students' self-esteem in the classroom is now recognised as a way of developing their capacity for learning, but scant attention is paid to the emotional cost to students of permitting growth and change. This script allows them to explore the feelings that go along with the experience of growth. There is a degree of manipulation in the script to make it a positive, rewarding experience.

> Take a moment or two to slow down your breathing.... As your breathing slows and you begin to relax, imagine that you are in a garden.... In this garden there is a rose bush.... Imagine you are the rosebush.... Feel your roots in the earth.... Be aware of your stem and your leaves.... Do you have thorns on your stem?.... At the very top of your stem, there is a rosebud, still closed and protected by a green covering.... Build up the feeling that in a moment your rosebud will slowly begin to open.... As the green covering folds back, be aware of the folded petals of the bud inside.... Now as the plant, let your rosebud open.... How do you feel?.... Feel the warmth of the sun as the petals open and fold back.... Feel the bud open fully to the light and the sun and the air.... Take a few moments to breathe in the light and air.... Allow your lungs to open and be filled with air.... As you breathe in, perhaps you can smell the perfume of the rose.... Breathe deeply and let yourself extend and expand.... As the rose opens fully so begin to open yourself.... Open your eyes and stretch.... Breathe a little more deeply.... Slowly, when you are ready, return to the room.

This script involves a combination of the students' being the rose in imagination and experiencing the feelings in their bodies as they 'allow the lungs to open and fill with air'. Here the connection between imagery and bodily experience is made explicit in the script. During the processing of the fantasy, the students often make the link spontaneously for themselves.

A more extended form of this fantasy involves inviting the fantasiser to go into and explore the rose.

THE FLEDGLING

The development of a fledgling can be construed as analogous to the development of the child from total dependence on the parent to independent functioning. In the light of this construction, it is important for the teacher not to put a value upon any of the stages of growth that the fledgling undergoes. If students pick up that the teacher feels that it is better to fly than to be in the egg, they are likely to devalue their own feeling if they preferred being in the shell.

Take two deep breaths and allow your body to relax.... Just let the tension go.... Imagine that you are looking down into a nest which contains some bird's eggs.... Where is the nest exactly?.... What does it look like?.... How many eggs are there in the nest?.... Now I want you to imagine that you are inside one of the eggs, curled up like a baby bird that is about to be born.... How do you feel curled up inside the egg?.... What is it like inside the shell?.... Now try knocking against the shell with your beak.... See how long it takes before you start to crack the shell.... As the shell begins to break some light begins to come in.... See how it feels as the shell breaks open and you can stretch out.... What are you like as a young bird that has just come out of its shell?.... Give yourself a good stretch.... Now you have grown up a little and it is time for you to fly for the first time.... Stand on the edge of the nest and stretch your wings.... How do you feel about the prospect of flying for the first time?.... Take a deep breath and take off.... See how it feels.... Fly round the nest and then go back to the edge of the nest and rest for a moment.... Now set off again and experiment with your flying.... Swoop around, glide and turn.... Fly high up into the sky until the nest is just a speck far below.... Go anywhere you want.... Do anything that you want.... Now become yourself again and watch the bird for a while.... Now have the sense that you are going to say goodbye to the fledgling and when it is right for you, breathe a little more deeply and gently begin to come back to the room.

THE FOUNTAIN

Feelings in classrooms are often allowed to build up because there is no legitimate means of expressing them. Invariably, when the feelings are released the cathartic effect produced is a disturbing one. Thus the mythology develops that expressing feelings is not permissible. 'The Fountain' script is one that allows students to recognise the build-up of feelings and experience the release with a positive cathartic effect.

Take two deep breaths and allow your body to relax.... Just let the tension go.... Imagine you are in a place and in this place there is a fountain which isn't working at the moment.... Take a good look at the fountain and what is around it.... What do you feel about this place?.... Now take a closer look and notice that a small amount of water is starting to come out of the fountain, but it is not very strong yet.... In imagination, see what it is like to be the trickle of water.... Become the water right now.... What does it feel like?.... Are you warm or cold?.... Now as the water, feel your pressure begin to build.... Feel the surge of energy as the pressure of the water begins to build and you flow faster and faster and are thrown up higher and higher.... How do you feel as you go higher and higher into the air?.... What do you look like right now?.... Just enjoy the sensation for a few moments.... Now let the flow of water gradually subside and become a trickle once again.... Feel the difference in your body.... As you become more aware of your body, breathe a little more deeply and gently come back to the room.

EXPANDING

Find a comfortable place to sit or lie and take three deep breaths.... For a while, just become aware of each breath.... Now have the sense that with each breath your neck is extending.... Your shoulders are expanding and the whole of the area around the neck and shoulders is becoming larger.... Your arms are lengthening and extending.... As you breathe your legs are becoming longer and more hollow.... Just continue to be aware of the breath and continue to allow the body to expand.... As the body expands, the spine lengthens.... As the spine lengthens, energy is released in the body, filling the spaces.... The body expands and fills with energy.... Find a way of releasing the energy in any way that seems right for you.... How are you feeling right now?.... Now build up the feeling that your body is slowly becoming its normal size again.... Breathe a little more deeply and gently come back to the room.

This script is highly effective as a means of inducing a relaxed state although there is no guarantee that it will work for every member of a group. In the post-fantasy discussion it could be worthwhile focusing on parts of the body that students found difficult to expand in imagination. This might be an indication of stress or chronic tension in that area. The next fantasy could have as its central theme relaxing 'the tense part'. Certainly this fantasy could have positive benefits in sport when too much tension can inhibit performance.

Chapter Eight

PROJECTION

We have made the connection between elements of scripted fantasy and parts of the personality. For subject areas, like Personal and Social Education, that aim to deal specifically with notions of self-identity and interpersonal relationships, the use of scripted fantasy can make an important contribution to that understanding of the self. The methodology differs quite radically from programmes of PSE that we have sometimes seen in operation in schools: page after page of photocopied material, hurriedly assembled, with little apparent understanding of the deeper psychological processes underlying an exploration of the self. This is not to criticise an already overburdened, overstressed and highly dedicated group of professionals but to offer instead a technique for both the teacher and student which employs a more creative approach to self awareness.

Crucial to an understanding of the self through the use of scripted fantasy is the notion of projection. This is a specific psychological term used to describe the process whereby an individual ascribes her own characteristics, construed either positively or negatively, to other individuals, animate or inanimate objects, events or images in a manner that denies an awareness of that connection. The term 'projection' is generally subsumed under the broader heading of 'defence mechanisms'.

We will illuminate the reader's understanding of the notion of projection using the following example of scripted fantasy. You may wish to try this with another adult to enhance personal learning or with a group of students.

CHOOSE AN OBJECT

Take two deep breaths and take a few moments to relax.... Take a good look around the room.... Now choose to focus your attention on any object you like in the room.... Take a good look at the object.... Note its size.... Shape.... Colour.... Texture.... Smell.... What is it used for?.... How old is it?.... What do you think life is like for the object?.... In imagination, see what it is like to be that object.... It might help if you closed your eyes now.... Don't just see the object in imagination, become the object right now.... You are this object.... What can you see?.... What can you hear?.... What is going on around you?.... See what it feels like to be this object.... What is your life like?.... In imagination, tell the other objects in the room what life is like for you and how you are treated.... What do you feel about that person who is looking at you?.... What is the best thing about being this object?.... What is the worst thing about being it?.... What will your life be like in the future?.... Now let the images fade and breathe a little more deeply.... When it feels right for you, gently come back into the room.

If you use this exercise with a group of students, you could then ask them to share their experience in pairs or in slightly larger groups. It can be helpful to ask the students to write about it before they talk, either as a piece of creative writing or as a response to some specific questions about the experience. Most students will have had an experience that makes sense to them and will be able to write about it coherently. The writing can then be shared in the groups as a stimulus for discussion.

As a clock: 'I am stiff and mechanical. I just keep going and can never stop.'

As a window: 'No one can see me. I am transparent and invisible even when people look straight at me. I can feel the cold wind and weather pressing against me.'

As a doormat: 'I am getting trodden on and crushed – people leave their dirt all over me.'

As the light: 'I am useful and helpful to people and help them when they can't see.'

As an earring: 'I am decorative and nice to look at, but I've got a sharp point.'

Students' statements like these are made with a great deal of feeling and seem to fit the personalities concerned. Some students even say that they have learned new things about themselves, recognising characteristics they had previously repressed or denied. They appear to be projecting parts of themselves, perhaps parts they are not willing to acknowledge, onto the inanimate objects they have chosen. They may view these characteristics as positive or negative. Conversely, any teacher who has had experience of working on a PSE course designed to enhance self-esteem will recognise the difficulty in getting students to accept their positive attributes.

'Projection' is the term that is usually given to this process. This is often listed as a defence mechanism and is used as a defence against acknowledging both positive and negative aspects of the self. A student might say to a teacher: 'You hate me, you don't like me, you don't want me in your class.' The shock of hearing this from someone you have worked hard with might be softened when you realise she is expressing unacknowledged parts of herself. The students may be projecting feelings of hatred and dislike for themselves or pouring out a generalised hatred for authority figures. Understanding this process does not absolve the teacher from the responsibility of handling the interaction sensitively; it merely adds a new dimension to her appreciation of it. Alternatively, a student might say, 'I really like your lessons. You really make them interesting. You get us to work hard.' This type of comment usually comes from students who are interesting and work hard themselves.

The process of projection also generalises to the staffroom group. The colleague who makes a genuine effort to praise other members of staff and give them positive feedback invariably merits the same kind of feedback. This also applies to negative messages. Listen to what your more critical colleagues are saying and you may find that the criticisms they make of others may equally well apply to themselves. Just about everything that annoys you about other people is likely to be true of yourself. People will often project their own feelings in passing comments. You might be told, 'You look under the weather,' and 'You are looking fit and relaxed,' within the space of a few minutes. Invariably, the speakers are saying more about themselves than they are about your condition.

It is possible to produce the same projection effect with a simple fantasy exercise as shown below.

WHAT KIND OF WEATHER AM I?

Ask the group to have a paper and pencil to hand and give them the following instructions:

> Have a good look at me right now and imagine what kind of weather I am [the teacher]. Write down the first thing that comes into your head.

Then go quickly round the group and ask them what they have written down. Inevitably, you will get a wide range of possible weathers, many of them contrasting: warm, rainy, windy, calm, stormy, sunny and so on. This would suggest that the individual members of the group are saying more about themselves than about you. If you get a consistent response from most of the group such as 'cloudy', then perhaps they are saying something important about you. There is often a degree of truth in the projection.

Just as the weather changes, so too do our feelings and moods. If you repeat this exercise on another occasion you will invariably get a different pattern of response. However, if there is a consistent response from a particular student, this may reflect a long-term issue between you.

It is important not to think of projection as something that is permanent or static. Below are two points that need to be considered:

1. Any projection relates only to one aspect of the individual. Take the 'imagining yourself to be an object' exercise. All the examples of responses given could have come from the same person. In fact they did, as they were generated by one of the writers, and all of the personal statements could represent his

current emotional concerns. In the case of the earring, there were seemingly conflicting statements produced, being both good to look at and yet having a sharp point.

2. Any projection relates to one point in time. As we have shown, there may be a consistency of response but it is important to bear in mind that this may not always be the case.

Many adults and children label themselves in ways that are restrictive with phrases like 'I am the kind of person who is untidy', 'I'm awful at maths', or 'I'm badly organised'. Sometimes these statements are true and sometimes they are not. The point we are making about projection challenges this kind of rigid labelling and offers the individual the possibility that there are many more choices in life. The individual is provided with the opportunity to see herself from many points of view.

How do psychological notions of projection relate to using imagery and scripted fantasy in the classroom? We would contend that fantasy provides a way of understanding the process of projection more clearly. By inferring personal meaning from the images generated by the fantasy, this process is opened up for examination. Psychologists have devised standard tests to encourage the process of projection and to make it public. The best known of these projection tests is the Rorschach Ink Blot Test. A number of random designs are used, made by spilling ink onto sheets of paper. These are then folded while the ink is still wet. The test is usually employed in a clinical setting and a client is asked to say what can be seen in the patterns. Her responses are analysed according to a fixed system of interpretation to determine her underlying psychological problems. One of the writers saw the skeletons of prehistoric monsters in some of the blots and was told he had a morbid personality. This form of fixed interpretation goes against the spirit of the view we are presenting here.

These standardised projection tests do not permit people to make sense of their own projections; neither would they ever be encouraged to do so by the professionals who employ them. Projection tests have developed out of a deterministic psychoanalytic tradition in which the interpretation of individual behaviour is firmly in the hands of the expert. Despite the fact that the use of imagery also evolved out of this tradition, with the work of Jung and Assagioli, it has come to be employed largely within a humanistic framework, in which the individual is encouraged to take responsibility for making sense of her own experience. The images generated by a scripted or guided fantasy provide one of the clearest forms of projection. Students and teachers report being startled by the way the images reflect important themes in their lives. The fantasy directs attention to such issues and presents them with unusual clarity. We believe that, at either a conscious or unconscious level, the individual is already aware of these issues, but may be unwilling or unable to look at them directly. For example, a middle-aged teacher attending an in-service course was taken through a fantasy of being a bird in a cage. The bird that emerged out of his fantasy was a mechanical one. He was taken aback by this image but readily offered the interpretation that this was how he felt inside. His emotional life had become mechanical and sterile and he felt incapable of spontaneity. The power of the experience to bring hidden or repressed feelings to the surface, meant that for this individual, he was able to talk about ways in which he might begin to change his behaviour.

Forging links with the unconscious need not be a concern for the teacher in the classroom, as the teacher is not there to be a therapist for the students. Although working as a clinician with disturbed children, Violet Oaklander (1978) provides moving examples of the therapeutic effects of fantasy. In her book, *Windows to Our Children*, she describes how to move to an understanding that fantasy does indeed reflect underlying emotional concerns. In response to a child's narrative account of a fantasy, she will use questions like: 'Is there anything like that in your life?'

When properly timed, an intervention of this nature can produce highly personal self-disclosure. As a teacher, perhaps in an educational setting such as a PSE lesson, it is important not to embarrass, upset or betray the trust of any student by making such a potent intervention in an unsuitable environment. Students should always be reminded to talk only about what feels right for them and should never be put under any pressure to disclose information of a personal nature which they are not fully ready to share. Building trust in a group as large as the conventional secondary school class is a fragile process. Used sensitively, scripted fantasy can do much to enhance relationships and engender trust. If, however, a teacher behaves in a crass or insensitive way with the feelings of students, then that trust will undoubtedly be put at risk.

Thus unwrapping projection can enable the individual to learn more about herself and the way in which she communicates with others. From a scientific point of view, one of the problems raised by the notion of projection is that there is no way of proving, in a rigorous empirical manner, that the process is actually taking place. The concept developed from the accumulated insights of psychiatrists working with their patients. The evidence for projection is therefore the accumulation of individual experience, something that is not highly valued by the psychological establishment. Most people who have worked with fantasy become convinced that they are projecting aspects of themselves into their imagery. They are, in effect, interpreting their fantasy experience for themselves.

The practice of interpretation can be an empowering one for the individual as it promotes self-awareness and encourages an ongoing critical examination of the self in relation to others. This self-empowering process can be reversed in the classroom if teachers unwittingly offer interpretations of elements contained within the students' fantasies. We would make the strong caveat that teachers should at all times resist the temptation to interpret what students report out of their experience of scripted fantasy. Part of the covert message received via the interpretation may be the denial of the students' phenomenological experience. Thus a drawing of a crying child hugging a doll produced by an unhappy-looking adolescent might prompt the superficial analysis that the student needs to regress to cope with present unhappiness in her life. Whether or not the interpretation is accurate is an irrelevance: the basic issue is about the power relationship that exists between students and teachers. The undeniable authority inherent in the role of teacher can cause the student to distort her perceptions in order to match those created for her by the authority figure. This dynamic is re-enacted countless numbers of times during the school day when black or female students have their experience constructed for them or denied by white or male teachers.

This process is also played out within the student peer group where hierarchies abound. It is the responsibility of the teacher therefore to discourage similar interpretations by the students during discussions of fantasy work. For those teachers working actively to promote the awareness of race and gender issues in schools, this is an important area to focus upon; that is, to work towards accepting the notion that each individual has a right to her unique perception of the world.

When is interpretation a valid activity? Certainly the idea of projection implies that the contents of fantasies are amenable to interpretation. Virtually every word we use has associations, but once again, within the context of using scripted fantasy in the classroom, we would advocate that only the student interpret her own experience. The following exercise may help to make this clear.

BRICK OR A STONE

Ask the class to form pairs.

Without telling your partner, decide on your answer to the following question: 'If you could be a brick or a stone, which would you rather be?' When you have both decided, you may tell each other. In the pairs, only one of you can be a brick and only one of you can be a stone. You may already agree but you will have to negotiate if you have both chosen the same object.

Then divide the class into groups of four or five, all of whom are bricks or stones. Ask them to discuss what being a brick or stone is like for them.

Invariably, this exercise brings out a range of associations, feelings and meanings for those who identify with either the bricks or stones. Sometimes the feelings are so strong against being either a brick or a stone that some individuals, including teachers on inservice courses, will strongly resist taking on a particular category.

Given the range of associations that emerge, exercises of this nature provide clear evidence that it is not appropriate to make general interpretations for specific images. You can produce the same effect by asking a group simply to brainstorm their associations with a word such as 'brick'. In two minutes we have come up with:

crumbling	beautiful
artificial	solid
block	man-made
dense	boring

no identity	a 'great' person
sharp-edged	a part of a whole
regular	undelineated

There has been a long tradition in psychiatry of making general interpretations for specific images, which effectively turns the images into symbols. Freud's forms of interpretation are of this nature and he offers interpretations of dream symbols that are related to sexual organs or sexual activity. This may be saying more about Freud's concerns than about dream imagery itself.

We have already suggested that it is inappropriate to make general interpretations that apply to more than one person. It is interesting that both psychiatrists and fortune-tellers find fixed methods of interpretation convenient methodologies for diagnosing and summing up others and their life experiences. This approach is the opposite of our suggestion that each individual evolves a set of meanings for her fantasy world which is unique to her. We would go even further and say that the only person who can make a meaningful interpretation is the person who has undergone the fantasy.

Letting go of the power to make interpretations may seem a risky business for teachers used to interpreting reality for whole classes of students and controlling the learning process. Below are examples of interpretations by teachers based, in the main, on their perception and interpretation of reality.

> This group is out of sorts today.
> You don't value each other enough in this group.
> You haven't learned anything.
> Now you know how mountains are formed.
> We've all enjoyed that, haven't we?

What then is the role of the teacher if she is to give up the conventional and accepted behaviour as the arbitrator of the norms within the classroom? We would suggest that the role of the teacher is to train herself and the students in the skills of attending, listening without judging or distorting, and reflecting back both the cognitive and affective elements contained within the students' reports. This will provide a sound basis for the students to make their own interpretations and also recognise that each individual has an equal right to his or her perception of reality. Using scripted fantasy then can be a basis for developing anti-sexist, anti-racist attitudes in the PSE curriculum.

We can understand the urge to be interpretive as, in our experience, the process of guiding a group through a scripted fantasy involves having a parallel fantasy ourselves, based on the same material. It is tempting to interpret the imagery of others in terms of our own. However, this is not a legitimate activity. As we have stressed, all fantasy experiences are unique and therefore will engender differing emotional associations. It may be interesting to discuss points of commonality but it must be understood that the meaning remains differentiated.

Jung (1961) supports the non-interpretive view. He advocated permitting the person who has the fantasy to analyse it in her own terms, using the process of 'active imagination'. A painting, a dream or a fantasy would be used as a starting point. The person would then be encouraged to re-experience the imagery, to encounter and confront elements of the fantasy and engage them in conversation. Jung described this as experiencing the unconscious while awake. In his role as therapist, he would ask questions such as, 'What occurs to you in connection with that?', 'Where does that come from?' or 'How do you think about it?' The interpretations seemed to emerge of their own accord from the patient's replies and associations.

Paradoxically, in his other writings, Jung (1959) described a set of archetypal images with common meanings, which have developed through the human race in the past. These archetypes, based largely on work with adults, include:

1. The Shadow, which represents aspects of the unconscious within a person, sometimes referred to as the 'darker side'.
2. The Anima, which represents the female tendencies in a man.
3. The Animus, which represents the male tendencies in a woman.
4. The Self, which represents the fully developed and integrated person, and may even encompass the whole cosmos.

These images are value-free and can involve what are conventionally seen as good and bad aspects of a person.

The notion of archetypal images implies that there is a genetic basis to the images we produce in our fantasy lives, which is passed on down the generations. The form of the image will change with time and in different cultures, but the essence remains the same. It is easy to see this view from images for the Shadow. Sometimes the Shadow is seen as an embodiment of evil, as with the devil in Christianity; whereas in eastern traditions, the Shadow is seen as integral to the total personality. This raises some important contemporary issues, such as the associations in western culture of good, white, male, rational; and evil, black, female, emotional and so on.

Assagioli (1965), in his book *Psychosynthesis*, suggested that interpretations could be made in terms of conflicts within the individual. Some images represent on the one hand inertia, laziness and a tendency to preservation, as opposed to growth, self-assertion and adventure on the other. This is probably an extremely important dimension. One of the writers (Hall, 1983) found that a high proportion of the images produced out of fantasy journeys by adults were perceived along this continuum.

Although we have cautioned against making interpretations of the images of another person, such interpretations may be correct, though there is no way of proving this. We have suggested that the hidden agenda in making interpretations may be to do with controlling the other person. Making an interpretation is similar to the traditional notion of teaching: that the task of the teacher is to tell the student what the world is like. If students are allowed to come to their own conclusions about the meaning of their imagery, then this is an important way in which they are able to take control of their own lives. After all, if they were to report their imagery to two experts with two differing theoretical models, they would probably receive two different interpretations! Far better to learn the skill of making interpretations for yourself.

Important strategies for enabling this process to take place are taken from the *Gestalt* techniques devised by Fritz Perls. This *Gestalt* methodology was introduced in the section on management issues and is discussed in detail by Passons (1975) in relation to counselling in schools, and by Hall and Hall (1988) in relation to work in the classroom. This is a method of facilitation that encourages students to examine their own imagery without any of the concomitant problems of interpretation, manipulation or distortion by the questioner. This approach can be used with students of all ages, including the very young.

Four characteristics of *Gestalt* theory are useful in the educational context:

1. Avoid questions beginning with 'why', because they require reasons, motives and explanations for behaviour to which the student may not have direct or immediate emotional access. 'Why' questions can also be perceived as interrogatory, so that the student may become bound up in feelings that have more to do with the questioner than with the question itself. Concentrate instead on questions beginning with 'what', 'how', 'when' and 'where'. These invite open, descriptive responses that encourage the student to talk at greater length.
2. Encourage students to personalise statements by using the first-person 'I', rather than 'you', 'we', 'one' or 'it'. This may appear to be a simple suggestion but one that often creates a great deal of difficulty. Perls argued that by distancing, disowning, splitting off or adopting similar strategies to avoid ownership of feelings, the individual cuts herself off from important aspects of her own personality. By personalising statements – perhaps using sentence stems such as: 'I feel/ felt ... when....' – the student is effectively coming to a much clearer understanding of the relationship between the emotional subtext and the content of what she is saying. The understanding of this relationship is central to the process of making personal interpretations.
3. Invite the students to take on the role of elements contained within their own fantasies. This process can be built into the script itself as in the fantasy 'The Park' from the 'Case History of a Lesson' (Chapter One):

> Now in imagination, see if you can become the friend.... What is it like to be the friend?.... As this imaginary friend, is there anything you would like to say?

During the subsequent discussion with a partner, the student can be encouraged to talk about what emerged out of this role reversal. Taking on the role of the image invites a far more thorough examination and it may be that students spontaneously reach the conclusion that they are saying something important about themselves, or even become aware of issues that were only partially understood or completely hidden.

4. Adopt a neutral tone of voice when reading the script aloud or talking to students about their fantasy experience.

This advice can be offered to students so that when they listen to each others' fantasies, they avoid the problems of judgementalism, sarcasm, put-downs and cynicism. This neutral tone also makes the process of owning and accepting parts of the self more of a possibility.

PARTS OF THE SELF

We have already suggested that elements in a fantasy may represent parts of the personality of the fantasiser. In just one fantasy there may be many different elements with which the individual can identify. In fact, every minute detail of the fantasy could be explored in the ways that we have suggested. It is possible to focus on images ranging from a desert to a grain of sand.

We are probably aware of different facets of ourselves, some more dimly than others. In different situations with different people at different times we may be lazy or energetic, defended or open, fearful or brave, cruel or kind. This supports the notion of parts of the self.

There is a part of me that wants to sit around and watch TV all day and another part that wants to be doing energetic things in the open air.

You may be familiar with this type of apparently contradictory feelings. What is less common is to accept them as being different but having equal validity as parts of the self. We do not wish to give the impression that we would support giving free rein to the less socially and personally desirable traits, such as our violence or greed. But unless we admit their existence, examine how far they affect our behaviour and understand their antecedents, they cannot be brought under our conscious control and may break out in unfortunate ways.

The educational value of exploring the many different aspects of the self is that it provides greater insight into our personal functioning and may even bring us into contact with resources and strengths that we can value, develop and use. One of the aims of the PSE curriculum is to enhance students' self-esteem and in our experience it is not only the negatively construed aspects of the self that are denied but also the positive ones. Teachers are discovering for themselves the difficulties of putting students in touch with their positive qualities with pupil profiling, self-assessment schedules and 'can-do' criteria. Helping students recognise, let alone acknowledge a personal quality can be a salutary experience. This problem is not the sole province of the student. Teachers themselves find it hard to look at and share their personal qualities and label the activity as an indulgence or an ego-trip. This somewhat puritanical mentality has far-reaching consequences when teachers are asked to appraise and evaluate their own professional strengths and weaknesses.

We would contend that using scripted fantasy as a means of discovering parts of the self, construed positively or negatively, can be the first step towards a realistic self-assessment and also the basis for goal-setting and appropriate behavioural or attitudinal change.

What are these parts of the self and how do we set about recognising them? Some psychologists refer to these parts of ourselves as subpersonalities. There is a problem with this term as it implies that there are several people contained under one skin and that they are fixed entities locked in time and space. We would argue that these subpersonalities are actually ongoing processes, feelings and emotions, which blend into each other and are continually changing.

Eva Fugitt (1983) worked with young students in the classroom, encouraging them to make lists of the various ways that they behaved in real-life situations. She then asked them to ascribe names to these different parts. The students produced such examples as:

I have a jealous Jenny.
I have a reading Ruth.
I have a part which is called Miss Laughing Hyena.
I have a part which likes to eat a lot called Fat Dumpling.

We can come to a cognitive understanding that there are seemingly conflicting parts of ourselves by identifying the situations in which these parts are called into play. For example, if you find that you behave in a shy, rather anxious manner when you meet people for the first time, this may seem to be at odds with other situations in which you feel confident and assertive. In an affective context, by accepting that neither the shyness nor the assertion represent the whole picture, it may be possible to be more objective about aspects of behaviour and begin the process of getting in touch with the emotional antecedents of that behaviour. Fugitt argues that this distancing shows students that they have more than one behavioural choice in a situation, which is empowering.

This approach cuts across the labelling of both students and teachers in educational institutions. Students are academic or non-academic, bright or lazy, noisy or quiet. Teachers are competent or ineffectual, good disciplinarians or too liberal, good communicators or poor communicators. This unidimensional labelling helps to reinforce notions that personality is fixed and change is unlikely. It is this tendency to set personality in concrete that is a self-defeating, destructive process militating against the possibility of change or growth. Conversely, the notion of subpersonalities permits both teachers and students to see themselves as a complex mix of qualities that can be either called into play or left in reserve, depending upon the perceived needs in any given situation. Certainly in the classroom, it may help students find a vocabulary for expressing this complex mix by using the sentence stem:

> There is a part of me which wants to ... and another part of me which wants to....'

Conflicting parts of the person are often represented in the imagery generated by a scripted fantasy. It is possible to build in a discussion between two elements of a fantasy into a script. Try the following example.

ANIMAL IN A ZOO

Make yourself comfortable.... Take three deep breaths.... Relax.... Just let the tension go.... Now take the first image that comes to you of an animal in a zoo.... What type of animal is it?.... What is the cage like?.... In imagination, become the animal.... Don't see yourself as the animal; actually be the animal and see what that is like.... What does your cage look like from the inside?.... How do you feel about being in this cage?.... What is your keeper like?.... How do you feel about your keeper?.... Are there people around your cage?.... If there are, what are they doing?.... How do you feel about these people?.... Now in imagination become the cage.... How do you feel as the cage?.... What do you think of this animal inside you?.... See if you have something to say to this animal, anything that comes.... Now become the animal and see if you have anything to say to the cage, anything that comes.... Become the cage again and reply.... Become the animal and talk back.... Now, as the animal, find a way of escaping from your cage, go anywhere you like.... How do you feel about escaping?.... What are the people in the zoo doing now?.... Just let the fantasy take you anywhere you want.... Now in fantasy, find a way back to your cage.... If you have made it back, see how you feel right now about being back inside the cage.... When it is right for you, find a way of saying goodbye to the animal and the cage.... Breathe a little more deeply and slowly come back to the room.

A scripted fantasy that asks students to adopt different roles and even become an animal can be considered as advanced and best attempted when the teacher is familiar with the technique. The 'Animal in a Zoo' would be an appropriate fantasy to use with older students working on issues in PSE to do with self-concept. By talking through the experience students may begin to discern ways in which they constrain themselves and feelings related to breaking out of these constraints can be explored. This can be a useful introduction to a discussion of the constraints placed upon individuals within society, thus raising important issues to do with gender, race, age, body-image and so on. However, it is important not to set expectations regarding the outcome of a fantasy. It may be that students do not want to move beyond the personal into wider social issues immediately and perhaps a subsequent lesson might address the issue of social constraints upon the individual.

With scripts that ask the student to become various elements in the fantasy, some guidelines may be needed to help process the subsequent discussion. We would suggest providing a list of key questions on cards such as:

Try to become the ... and see what that's like.

How do you feel as the ...?

What is your life like as the ...?

What advice would you like to give to the ...?

How do you feel about that?

For students working in pairs using a focused listening technique, these questions can encourage an in-depth examination of each other's material. Clearly the questions don't have to be used in this order, but it is important to point out that they are open-ended and not looking for a 'correct' response. In the next chapter we provide a collection of scripts that can be used to focus on specific aspects of the self.

Chapter Nine

PROJECTION SCRIPTS

The process of projection is almost certainly involved in the responses to all of the following fantasy scripts. For students, the feelings that emerge out of the experience may represent issues that are currently important for them in their lives, even though they may be unaware of the connection at that moment. The act of talking through the fantasy with a sensitive partner can help students gain important insights into patterns of behaviour that may be inappropriate or self-destructive. It is this process of reflection that can lead to self-determined attitudinal and behavioural change.

The likelihood is that there will be a correlation between the students' most potent projections and the major elements in the fantasies. Nevertheless, some students will choose idiosyncratic aspects of the script that happen to most suit their current psychological needs.

We try to resist the temptation to project our own concerns into the introduction to each fantasy, while realising that this is an unattainable goal. It would be virtually impossible to communicate ideas without some form of projection taking place.

THE GARDEN

The central theme of this fantasy script is discovering parts of the self that are positive but of which we remain unaware. We would suggest that this would be an effective fantasy for use in programmes of work designed to enhance self-esteem. Some suggestions for processing this fantasy are given at the end.

Take two deep breaths and allow your body to relax.... Just let the tension go.... Imagine that you are sitting in a room in a house.... As you sit you look out of the window into the garden.... The part of the garden near the house is carefully looked after.... Towards the end of the garden it begins to become untidy.... The plants are overgrown and grow so thickly that you can't see the end of the garden.... Take a good look at the tidy parts of the garden nearer to the house.... How are they set out?.... What sort of plants can you see?.... How do you feel about the tidy part of the garden?.... Now have a look at the overgrown part at the end of the garden.... What are the plants like here?.... What can you see in the distance?.... Try to look into the distant parts at the back of the garden.... Build up the feeling that there is a friendly animal living there, any animal you like.... What sort of animal is it?.... Perhaps you can catch a glimpse of it moving through the undergrowth.... How do you feel about the animal?.... Find a way of letting the animal know you are there.... In imagination, see if you can become this animal.... Look at the world through its eyes.... In imagination become the animal right now.... What is it like to be you?.... How are you feeling?.... What are your good qualities?.... What things do you do really well?.... Imagine that you can talk to the person who is looking out of the window.... Tell that person about your good qualities.... How could that person use the qualities that you have?.... Now become yourself again, looking out of the window.... How do you feel about your animal now?.... What do you feel about what the animal said to you?.... Now in imagination find a way of saying goodbye to your animal and the garden.... Breathe a little more deeply and when you are ready, gently come back to the room.

A key question to offer students when processing this fantasy might be: 'Do you share any of the qualities that the animal had?' This may lead into a discussion about personal qualities. If, however, they deny that they share any qualities in common with the animal, three further questions might be asked:

Did the animal have any qualities that you would like to have?

How might you set about acquiring these qualities?

114

PROJECTION

How would your life change if you had these qualities?

For many students this type of discussion can open up a way of talking about behaviour which hitherto they had not even construed as being positive. In this way the vocabulary for expressing aspects of self-esteem can emerge naturally and spontaneously.

THE TREE

In the chapter describing the effect of scripted fantasy on the quality of students' writing, examples were given of responses to a fantasy of being a tree. The tree seems to provide a potent image for expressing feelings that may previously have been repressed. This script has been used successfully with primary-age students and teachers report an unusually high degree of involvement in the activity of drawing the tree and then writing or talking about it. The writers have used it with teachers on in-service courses and students with special needs with similar results.

Take two deep breaths and allow your body to relax.... Just let the tension go.... Summon up an image of a tree.... It doesn't have to be a tree you know.... Try to make it your own tree.... What does it look like?.... What does the trunk look like?.... What are the branches and leaves like?.... What do you feel about this tree?.... Now in imagination, try to become the tree.... Don't see yourself as the tree, actually be the tree.... What can you see around you?.... Are there any people about?.... What is the weather like?.... Try to feel the temperature and any wind or breeze.... What does it feel like to be this tree?.... Now become aware of your trunk.... What is the outside of your trunk like?.... What does your bark feel like?.... What has happened to your bark over time?.... Now be aware of what is happening inside your trunk.... How are you feeling inside?.... What are your branches like and your leaves if you have any?.... How do you feel about your branches and leaves?.... Now go down into your roots.... What is happening down in your roots?.... How do you feel about your roots?.... Now step out of the tree and become yourself again.... Take a good look at the tree and be aware of your thoughts and feelings.... Now find a way of saying goodbye to your tree.... Breathe a little more deeply and when you are ready gently come back to the room....

Students can be asked to draw their trees and then write about the fantasy using the trigger phrase: 'I am the tree and I...' A variation of this fantasy is to go through the four seasons and emphasise the seasonal changes that the tree undergoes.

Vanessa Jones, a teacher on an in-service course at Nottingham University, has also used it as a way to explore feelings in a counselling situation with her nine-year-old daughter, Katherine. The fantasy was used on two occasions: first, when Katherine was emotionally upset, as a vehicle through which to verbalise the upset; and second, to review the situation a day or so later when the emotion seemed to have dissipated. Both felt that the fantasy had been a powerful tool to enable Katherine explore her feelings. Vanessa commented:

Katherine has decided to draw her feelings as trees on several occasions since, each time when she has had particularly strong feelings, either positive or negative. Her comments on this activity suggest that imagery can be very effective in developing self-awareness.

BIRD IN A CAGE

This script is more complex in that it invites students to take on the roles of two elements in the fantasy and then sets up a conversation between the two. This is more suitable for older students who have had some experience of fantasy work. It could be modified for younger students by removing the sections of dialogue between the bird and the cage. The central theme is about the difference between constraint and freedom and the feelings associated with these states. The post-fantasy discussion could legitimately be focused on two levels: the personal and the societal.

Take two deep breaths and allow your body to relax.... Just let the tension go.... Try to summon up an image of a bird in a cage.... Take the first image that comes and see what it is like.... What sort of bird is it?.... What size and colour is it and what type of feathers does it have?.... What is it doing now?....

Is it singing?.... How do you feel about this bird?.... Now take a good look at the cage.... What is it made of?.... What size and colour is it?.... How do you feel about this bird being in the cage?.... Now, in imagination, try to become the bird and experience what this feels like.... How do you feel about being in the cage?.... What is your life like?.... Now change and try to become the cage and experience what that is like.... What does it feel like to be the cage?.... What is your life like as the cage?.... What do you think about the bird which lives inside you?.... Now become the bird again and see if you have anything to say to the cage, anything that comes.... Begin by saying 'Cage ...' and just go along with the words that come.... Now become the cage again and reply to the bird and just go along with the words that come. 'Bird ...' Become the bird again and now in imagination find a way of getting out of the cage.... Just let it happen.... See what it feels like to be out of the cage.... Just let the fantasy go anywhere it wants.... As the bird, be aware of where you travel.... Now in imagination, find a way to get back to your cage.... If you want to go back to it, be aware of how you feel about being back there in the cage.... Have the sense that you can leave any time you want.... If you don't want to go back to it, be aware of how you feel right now.... Now begin to breathe a little more deeply and when you feel ready, bring your attention back to the room.

It is interesting to note that teachers and students who have experienced this fantasy report that they were able to feel the cage in terms of tension in their bodies. This points up the interrelatedness between psychological and physiological processes which we develop further in the discussion of right-brain functioning.

THE WISE PERSON

This fantasy is often given under the heading of 'The Wise Old Man', with the intention of generating imagery related to Jung's archetype. Far more choice is provided if the gender is unspecified, which also avoids the obvious trap of predetermining sex roles when dealing with imagery.

Take two deep breaths and allow your body to relax.... Just let the tension go.... Imagine that you are walking through the foothills of a mountainous area.... As you begin to climb upwards, take a good look at the scenery.... The trees and the mountains around you.... Be aware of the feelings in your body as you walk along the mountain path.... Breathe in the smell of the trees.... Stop for a moment and have a good look at the view.... Now as the path becomes steeper, it is more difficult to walk.... In places you have to scramble a little.... There is a fork in the path ahead.... Take the route that you know leads to a high valley.... Here, a wise person lives in a cave.... As you carry on along this branching path, the light begins to fade.... The shadows become darker and more mysterious and you can hear the sounds of wildlife in the bushes and among the rocks.... How do you feel about being here?.... Soon a bright moon comes out and now it is easier to find your way.... In the distance you can see the flickering light of a fire and you know that you must be near your destination.... As you come closer to the fire, it is possible to see the outline of the cave and the wise person sitting by the fire.... You go over to the fire and sit down. For a long time, no words are spoken.... Take a good look at your wise person.... Now, in imagination, become the wise person.... What does it feel like to be the wise person?.... What do you think of the person who has come to see you?.... Try talking to the person who has come to see you.... Give some advice that is right for the person right now.... When you have finished talking, reach into the folds of your clothes and take out a gift and give it to your visitor.... Now become yourself again, take your leave of the wise person and start on the journey back down the mountain.... How do you feel as you walk along?.... As you walk, take out your gift and examine it carefully.... Be aware of your feelings as you continue on your journey home.... In imagination, say goodbye to the wise person and the mountain.... Breathe a little more deeply and gently begin to bring your attention back to the room.

Although this is a long script, it can be extended by examining the gift in more detail.

When you arrive at the foot of the mountain, sit down at the side of the road and take out the gift.... Place it on the ground in front of you and take a good look at it.... Now pick up the gift and feel its weight.... What does the surface feel like?.... Can you guess the reason the wise person chose this gift for you?.... Now in imagination, become the gift and be aware of what that feels like.... As the gift, see if there is anything you would like to say to the person who is examining you.... Just say anything that comes.... Perhaps give them some advice.... Now become yourself again and put the gift back into the folds of your clothes.... How are you feeling as you set off to go home?....

There is far more scenic detail given in this fantasy than in any of the others provided. It is particularly effective as a stimulus for drawing or painting:

Choose an image from the fantasy which was most vivid for you. Represent it, using colours and textures which most powerfully convey that image.

This highly potent theme is more appropriate to introduce to a group of students who have some facility in talking about their own issues because of the potential for self-discovery contained within the script. Clearly, on one level it can be seen as a gift from the teacher to the class.

The impact of scripts such as these cannot be measured in cold print. In order to experience the range of feelings that can be generated by fantasy, it is necessary to try them out for yourself. Getting in touch with these feelings appears to produce an energising effect that is reflected in the sharing of experience in the post-fantasy discussions. It is this raw energy which many teachers find difficult to tap into in PSE lessons, leaving students emotionally untouched. Thus the possibility of self-discovery remains beyond the grasp of both student and teacher. Fantasy can provide the tools for building the connections between self-awareness, learning and change.

Chapter Ten

THE RIGHT BRAIN

Fantasy and imagery are processes often described in the psychological literature as being under the control of the right hemisphere of the brain. Conversely, the left hemisphere is thought to control activities such as language and rational thinking. Education in this country has been criticised in some quarters, notably by feminists and health educators, for placing a higher value on left-brain activities while devaluing right-brain activities, and there have been consistent attempts to make educational practice more integrated and holistic in its approach to learning. It must be admitted, though, that with the onset of the national curriculum and testing at seven, eleven and fourteen, such initiatives are bound to lose momentum unless teachers themselves take responsibility for giving students the opportunity to experience learning other than through a verbal mode.

A description of brain functioning illustrates how the split-brain hypothesis developed, but as Blakeslee (1980) points out, the brain is a much more complex organ than this simple model would suggest. Nevertheless, it still provides a useful metaphor to elucidate processes that are difficult to explain in any other terms. The split-brain hypothesis was developed out of Sperry's (1968) work with epileptic patients. The main part of the brain, or cortex, is in discrete halves joined together at the base by bundles of fibres called the corpus callosum. Sperry believed that if the corpus callosum was cut in half, epileptic seizures would be prevented from spreading from one half of the brain to the other. To all intents and purposes, these patients behaved normally after the operations. However, under experimental conditions it was shown that any information taken in by the left hand or the left field of the patients' vision could not be described in words. This information appeared to be decoded by the right brain and as there remained no physical connection with the left brain, the information could not be expressed in language.

The split-brain hypothesis was developed out of these experiments. The left brain appeared to control functions such as language, logic and calculation, which are all skills necessary for rational thinking. The right brain appeared to control functions such as intuition and pattern recognition, skills necessary for creative expression. Based on such findings, these sentences were initially typed on a word processor, with the screen deliberately placed to the left in order to stimulate the more creative functions of the brain!

In some individuals, the functions of the hemispheres are reversed. This may be connected to left-handedness, but is by no means always the case. If one hemisphere of the brain is damaged, then it is possible for the other to take on both functions. For most healthy individuals, however, these two sets of activities do seem to operate separately and may even interfere with the functioning of the other. For example, being emotionally upset may interfere with your ability to think rationally; alternatively being overly rational may inhibit your ability to get in touch with feelings.

This lack of connection between two sets of activities is perhaps best illustrated in the area of nonverbal communication. When in conversation, we have access not only to the spoken word but also to visual cues and intuitive feelings about the other person. Sometimes there appears to be a mismatch between what the person says and the nonverbal cues that are being given. Most of us, having undergone an education that emphasises left-brain activity, have a tendency to pay attention to verbal statements and may just be left with an uneasy feeling about the nonverbal, paralinguistic information we pick up. Counsellor training involves developing the skill of attending to the emotional subtext as well as to the meaning of the words. Young children appear to have this skill naturally and react according to their intuitive feelings. Parents of young children often remark on their offsprings' ability to pick up feelings, however well disguised. If, as psychologists suggest, 90 per cent of all communication is nonverbal, it would seem that the educational emphasis on left-brain activities is disproportionate.

What we choose to call the 'unconscious' may be information that can be accessed by the right brain but which we are unable to put into words. The visual arts are a logical outcome of this notion. In fact, the surrealist movement intentionally set out to make a connection between the unconscious and the visual. Scripted and guided fantasies also share this ability to access hidden material and raise it simply and clearly into consciousness via imagery. Having been brought into consciousness through the vehicle of fantasy, it can then be expressed through language. It is as if the material requires a vehicle other than words to make it accessible.

To summarise, we have linked a number of processes to right-brain activity: imagery involving all the senses, pattern recognition, intuition, creativity, relaxation and feeling. Almost all students and adults who have experienced a scripted fantasy report a sense of physical well-being and relaxation as well as a whole host of feelings. They also report having intuitive insights and creative solutions to personal problems. It seems a reasonable assumption that there is an underlying physiological basis to these linked processes.

The right brain accessed through the use of fantasy appears to have a vast potential that for most of us remains untapped. One way of releasing this potential is to develop our imaging capacity. Two areas where this is being used both creatively and systematically are in sport and alternative medicine.

IMAGERY AND SPORT

A volleyball team arrives for a morning training session. The coach asks them to lie down on the floor and in imagination journey to a beautiful place where they can enjoy the weather and the scenery. He knows that the fantasy experience will invariably produce a highly relaxed state in members of the team.

This may not be the type of training session we recall from our school days; the traditional approach to sport was to try hard, to train hard and push the body to its limits. Nowadays, coaches are just as likely to ask their teams to lie down and indulge in a fantasy experience to help them relax as part of a skills training programme. Syer and Connelly (1984) provide a number of practical strategies for using imagery to improve performance in a variety of sports.

They suggest using imagery to deal with two key issues related to performance: anxiety and tension. They provide a script designed to reduce anxiety levels by putting anxieties into a black box and leaving the box on a shelf. This is similar to the script given earlier, in which problems were put into a rucksack and left behind. Thoughts that run constantly through our minds are often bound up with success or failure in relation to past or future events. For sportspeople these evaluations can prove a distraction from the immediate task of performing a skill superlatively well. The controlled use of imagery can provide the means to blot out these distracting thoughts and at the same time relax the body, releasing tension which is not required to perform the relevant skill. For example, letting go of tension in the jaw has been demonstrated to improve performance in throwing the javelin.

Using fantasy for training purposes is not confined to the professional. A physical education teacher, Malcolm Dewell, employed fantasy to enable adolescents to learn the difficult skill of javelin throwing. We quote at length from a report of his interventions with a group of first-year students in a comprehensive school.

> The group sat around me on the school field. It was a pleasant, warm and sunny day. I showed the javelin to the group and then introduced the three different gripping techniques: finger and thumb, second finger and thumb and the nordic grip. I then demonstrated the grips and how to use them. The javelin throw can be broken down into four main sections: the grip, the point of release, the flight and the landing. Each of these sections was explained. I then began to introduce the fantasy element with each boy still sitting on the grass around me. I started to introduce a guided fantasy starting off with the group being aware of where they were, what they could feel, hear and smell around them. I then asked them to become one of the javelins which were lying on the ground around the group and asked them what it felt like to take the part of the javelin. I then took the fantasy through all of the stages of the javelin throw. What was it like to be picked up? How were you gripped? Where were you when the thrower carried you? What was it like at the point of release? I tried to involve as many senses as I could. We then progressed through the flight stage and the landing. I watched the group closely during the 'landing stage' and noticed that some of the boys gave an involuntary jolt. Perhaps feeling the bump as they landed! Not wanting to leave the

group in a state where they had just been thrown, I brought the group back to where they had started and got them to enjoy a few moments experiencing the peace and calm around them and then asked them to open their eyes. All through the guided fantasy I had left pauses so that they could spend time 'feeling' what it was like. At no time were they rushed at all.

Following this I did not question the group but went straight into the throwing of the javelin. Without any more teaching or coaching techniques the boys each started throwing the javelin. One thing which pleased me was that I could hear the boys talking, along the lines of 'which grip did you have?' This meant that the boys were talking together about how they had felt during their experience. A further point which I noticed was that, more than other groups, the boys seemed more aware of the constituent parts of the throw and were discussing each other's throws, techniques and performances. I have found in the past that I often need to go over various technicalities such as the grip or the point of release but this was not the case with this group. In general, they seemed to be aware of what was needed. Was this because they had experienced being the javelin themselves? At the end of the lesson I gave out 'questionnaires' and they were completed without, as far as possible, ideas being taken from the person alongside. After this was done I talked to the group about the imagery. The general consensus of feeling was that the fantasy was worthwhile and had helped them to grasp what was going on and made it easier to understand the technical aspects of the throw. A small percentage said they 'felt daft' – was it coincidence that these were the two boys who seemed not to understand the grip and felt that they were poor at throwing the javelin? Another feeling was that the fantasy had been too short – in fact it had taken eight minutes. Most of the boys now were talking freely about the fantasy and I felt that most of them had 'got into it' and hadn't had an image other than that of the javelin. On questioning some of the group who I had seen 'jolt' on landing, I found that they had indeed felt a bump and in some cases this was pointed up in the questionnaire.

In later sessions, the 'fantasy group' were able on average to throw the javelin further than two similar first-year groups who had not used imagery as part of training.

A further role for imagery in sport is the mental rehearsal of skills. In a relaxed state with the eyes closed, a single activity or a whole series of activities can be practised in imagination using as many sensory modalities as possible. It is claimed that time spent in mental rehearsal can be more effective than the same amount of time spent in the actual practice of a physical skill. Masters and Houston (1978) make the same claim for increasing flexibility using the fine movements suggested by Moshe Feldenkrais for integrating the body and the mind. Syer and Connelly (1984) were working with Tottenham Hotspur Football Club when the team were enjoying success in the early 1980s. It would be interesting to know if Tottenham had stopped using these techniques when their fortunes took a downward turn at a later date.

These suggestions involve the rehearsal of performance in the future. Imagery can be used to provide a mental replay of a recent or past performance. During the replay, minor adjustments can be made to improve performance at the next attempt. This would be particularly useful in an event like the high jump where there is a time interval between attempts at the bar.

Another application of imagery in sport is to employ an image that provides an analogy for the activity that has been chosen for improvement. One of the writers used the image of an antelope when he was going for long runs through wooded countryside. Syer and Connelly report the marksman who used an image of the Rock of Gibraltar in order to remain still while taking aim and firing. This form of imagery can be evoked as the activity is being performed. This method of employing imagery to improve performance is applicable in virtually every situation, from learning to drive a car to giving birth, from fighting disease to practising social skills. It is this particular aspect of using imagery that is most widely relevant across the school curriculum and the creative teacher can harness its power to improve cognitive, affective and social skills.

To date, there is still no body of empirical research that provides incontrovertible evidence justifying the use of imagery in sport. However, increasing numbers of athletes and their coaches are adopting techniques of this nature because they appear to work for them. Perhaps this provides the best form of evidence for such a hard-nosed group of people as professional athletes.

SELF-APPRAISAL AND MENTAL REHEARSAL OF FUTURE EVENTS AND SKILLS

In the previous section we referred to the mental rehearsal of physical skills in sport and how this was becoming common practice among athletes. The same technique can be used for all types of skills, including social skills. Projecting yourself imaginatively into one of the many life-roles you occupy, such as teacher, parent, student, confident socialiser and so on, can be used to rehearse those roles that at present may be problematic but that you may wish to gain more understanding of and control over.

Mental rehearsal is a technique that can be employed in a wide variety of educational settings. The most obvious of these, perhaps, is in the pastoral interview, when students are encouraged to look at aspects of their behaviour and acknowledge the implications of that behaviour for themselves and the institution. What many teachers with pastoral responsibility find less than easy to do in this situation is to find alternatives to coercion, threats, reward and punishment, cajolery and so on, to help students achieve self-determined behaviour change. Using imagery in the form of mental rehearsal can provide the bridge between knowing how the student wants to change and actually accomplishing the change.

The first step in this process is to isolate the variables in behaviour that are perceived by the student to be unhelpful. This can only be done by the individual but is obviously dependent to an extent on feedback from significant others such as fellow students, teachers and family. Let us take the example of an isolated student who finds initiating interactions with other students and members of staff extremely difficult. It may be that through an interview with a form tutor, head of year or school counsellor, the student identifies for herself that this inability to make relaxed social contact is causing personal unhappiness as well as difficulty with joining in work groups in class. If at this point the student expresses a desire to change, the teacher in the pastoral role can use the strategy of mental rehearsal to facilitate that change.

The second step is to bring the presenting problem into sharper focus. The student can be asked to recall a situation or situations in which the shy behaviour caused problems and made her wish that she could have behaved differently. Let us imagine that the student has found it difficult to ask the maths teacher for help when she hasn't understood a mathematical process. What she wanted to do was to put up her hand and say clearly, 'I need help, I haven't understood what you said.' In essence four significant variables have been elicited which are necessary for the mental rehearsal to be effective:

1. the time that the event took place;
2. the place in which it happened;
3. the person who was involved;
4. how exactly the student responded and how she would like to have responded.

A way of making the process more concrete is to encourage the student to write down specific responses to each of the four variables. If the student has limited writing skills, then a tape recording might be a helpful alternative. This establishes clear parameters for the new behaviour.

The third step is to take the student through a brief relaxation procedure. It is likely that, having asked the student to talk about difficult situations and feelings, there will be a residual tension or anxiety that may inhibit imaging. The relaxation allows the student the opportunity to release stress, let go of feelings and lead naturally into the mental rehearsal.

MENTAL REHEARSAL FOR PERSONAL EFECTIVENESS

Make yourself comfortable in your chair.... It may help if you sit fairly straight, with your feet flat on the floor and your hands relaxed in your lap.... Try to breathe a little more deeply.... If it feels right, close your eyes.... Perhaps allow the breathing to deepen a little more.... Imagine that you are breathing in relaxation and breathing out tension.... Be aware of the pressure of your body on your chair.... Just relax and enjoy the sensation that you have nothing to do right now.... Now try to stay relaxed as you bring up an image of a maths lesson.... What is happening in the room around you?.... Take a good look.... What can you hear in the room?.... How do you feel about being there?.... Don't see yourself in the room, actually be there, looking through your own eyes.... Now imagine that you are working on a maths problem and you have no idea of what to do.... Try to stay relaxed and be aware of how you are feeling right now.... Build up the feeling that you are going to ask for help and that it will be all right.... In imagination, put your hand up.... Now let Mrs X ask you what you want.... Feel yourself clearly and confidently saying the words.... Have a sense of calm and relaxation as Mrs X replies.... Stay with the feeling of confidence and relaxation as the discussion between you continues.... Try thanking Mrs X and feel that if you ever need help again it is OK to ask for it.... Bring the feelings of confidence and relaxation back into the room as you breathe a little deeper and open your eyes.

There has been a strong affirmation of positive feelings written into this script. The associations that emerged out of a successful interaction in imagination can be used as the basis for a positive mental set when next the student meets a difficult situation. At this stage it becomes important to encourage the student to target a time and place in which the intervention can be tried out in reality. This procedure may have to be repeated at intervals, when success has been gained and the student feels ready to move on to other situations that create emotional difficulties. It may be possible to ensure that the first attempt meets with success if the support of Mrs X is enlisted. Subsequent interviews might include a review of the intervention, the results that ensued and the feelings that emerged. Progressively more difficult situations can be negotiated until the degree of personal effectiveness the student desires has been attained.

So far we have limited the discussion of mental rehearsal to the one-to-one counselling interview. However, shyness and personal effectiveness are issues that affect most adolescents and the technique can be adapted for use with whole groups in the classroom. Coping with the problems of transfer from primary to secondary school or preparing for job interviews are just two examples where mental rehearsal can prove effective. Special needs students can also derive enormous benefit from mental rehearsal of simple skills, like using a vending machine or negotiating a route around school, and an appropriate version of these instructions can be used.

Having raised the issue of social skills or shyness with a class, perhaps in the context of a form tutor period or a PSE lesson, most students will be able to identify people and situations with which they have difficulty in coping. It may be helpful to encourage them to share their feelings about such situations first, perhaps discussing them in the safety of pairs. This sharing by itself is probably a helpful activity, which can be reinforced by a short fantasy activity, an example of which we give below. It is as important to spend time relaxing a group of students as it is in the one-to-one interview. This relaxation process will help to ensure that the students do not experience undue anxiety when they practise the non-shy behaviour in imagination. After the relaxation you might begin.

DEALING WITH SHYNESS

Now you are relaxed, I want you to summon up an image of
a time in your life when you felt shy.... Take a good look
round.... Are there any people?.... What exactly is going
on?.... How are you feeling?.... Now in imagination, I want
you to build up the feeling that you are going to behave in a
different way.... Now let a feeling of confidence start to grow
in your body and allow the feeling to spread throughout your
body.... Now start to behave in a confident way.... What are
you doing?.... What are you saying?.... How do you feel
now?.... How do other people respond to you?.... Give yourself permission to do whatever you want to do.... As the images fade remember that whenever you need to feel
confident you can recall the feeling at any time.... Don't lose
this feeling of confidence as you gently come back to the
room.

Again, it is important to build success into this kind of mental rehearsal or students will merely end up reinforcing a debilitating
habit. By mentally practising a situation that normally produces
anxiety in a relaxed manner, the individual stands a better chance
of reducing that anxiety. This is a process that psychologists call
'desensitization'.

The example of shyness can be developed more fully with the
group using the technique of goal-setting similar to the method
used in the counselling interview. This procedure encourages stu-

dents to be far more specific about an aspect of behaviour that is to be practised in the future. The goal should be both realistic and achievable, defined in clear, simple terms, including the time and place that the behaviour will be tried out. A simple example might be to compliment someone. As each of the students will probably have chosen a different item of behaviour to try out, a much more open form of mental rehearsal would have to be used.

ATTAINING YOUR GOAL

Now you are relaxed and comfortable, summon up an image of the scene just before the behaviour you want to try out.... What is going on?.... What are you doing?.... How are you feeling?.... Now, in imagination, try out your goal.... How are you feeling now?.... How does the other person respond?

One aspect of shyness is the inability to self-disclose information or talk about feelings. Appropriate self-disclosure is often described as a social skill and this is another subject that is suitable for mental rehearsal. In this script students are asked to do two things: first, to go through the process of self-disclosure; and second, to talk about it afterwards, a second-order form of self-disclosure.

SELF-DISCLOSURE

Settle down in your chair and begin to relax.... Take a couple of deep breaths and be aware of letting go of the tension in your body.... In imagination, think of someone who you would like to share feelings with, but at the moment find it difficult.... These feelings might be about something that happened recently, or an event from a long time ago.... In imagination, build up the sense that you are going to share these feelings with that person.... Actually be there and look through your own eyes.... In imagination, meet this person.... Now let a feeling of confidence fill your whole body as you begin to share your feelings with the person.... Let the other person respond.... How are you feeling right now?.... Now let those images fade.... I want you to imagine that you are in a group of three or four people from this class and you are telling them what happened in your fantasy.... What do you say?.... How do you feel as you are talking?.... How do the other people react?.... Let the conversation develop naturally.... Let those images fade as you breathe a little more deeply and begin gently to come back to the room....

Now form groups of three or four and take turns in sharing what came up during the fantasy. You don't have to talk about people or events if you don't want to, but try to express some of the feelings that emerged during the fantasy.

Having undergone a mental rehearsal of self-disclosure, even those students who find talking about feelings difficult report that they are beginning to share almost despite themselves. Some students actually disclose the memory for the first time and it ceases to have the importance it had when it was kept inside. One student self-disclosing will often trigger off self-disclosures in the others. It is, however, important to make clear that secrets can be kept. Self-disclosure of this nature can have an emotionally releasing effect for a group and create an atmosphere of trust and caring built on an empathic understanding of each others' life experience.

The usefulness of mental rehearsal is not confined to the schoolroom. Here is an example of mental rehearsal we have employed with groups of up to 60 teachers as part of in-service courses on interpersonal skills. With modifications, these same techniques could be used with PSE groups in schools.

GIVING FEEDBACK

The procedure involves giving the following instructions:

Write down three things that you have not said before and that you would like to say to (a) a colleague, (b) your headteacher, and (c) a student's parent. Even though they may be emotionally charged comments for you, try to ensure that you phrase them skilfully and that they would not block the person concerned from making a response.

Now relax, and when you feel comfortable, close your eyes and take three deep breaths.... Imagine that you are in school walking down the corridor towards the staffroom.... As you go into the staffroom you can see your colleague sitting in a chair.... As you go over and sit down next to her or him build up the feeling that you are going to say something.... Check that you are relaxed and breathing comfortably.... Now say what you want to say to your colleague.... How does your colleague respond?.... Just let the dialogue develop naturally.... How are you feeling right now?....

Let those images go, and shift the scene.... Leave the staffroom and walk towards the headteacher's room.... Check that you are relaxed and breathing comfortably.... Go into the room and greet the headteacher.... Build up the feeling that you are going to say something important.... Now say what you want to say.... How does the headteacher respond?.... Just let the dialogue develop naturally.... How are you feeling?....

Let those images go, and shift the scene to a time when you meet the students' parents.... Imagine that the parent you would like to make a statement to is coming into your room.... Check that you are relaxed and that you are breathing comfortably.... Build up the feeling that you are going to say something important.... Now say what you want to say.... How does the parent respond?.... Just let the dialogue develop naturally.... How are you feeling right now?

The inability to say what we want to say when we want to say it is a continual source of stress in personal and professional relationships (Hall and Hall, 1988). Many teachers report storing up feelings over long periods of time which either become explosive or leak out in inappropriate or destructive forms. Certainly, using mental rehearsal as a vehicle for discussing what prevents you from saying these things to these people can provide valuable insights into your own behaviour. It may be that the fantasy is a way of breaking down habitual patterns of response that are ineffective in your present situation. Some people, however, report that a single mental practice can be very effective in bringing important emotional issues to the surface.

HEALING

Imagery has become very fashionable in alternative medicine and the suggestion has even been made that the symptoms of cancer can be ameliorated by the use of imagery. This idea has been given prominence by the work of Simonton, Matthews-Simonton and Creighton (1980). Their work is still very controversial amongst the medical establishment and their detractors would claim that they are giving false hope to cancer patients.

As part of the anti-cancer therapy, the authors encouraged their patients to relax and then use imagery to represent the white blood cells destroying the cancer cells, which were then flushed out of the system in imagination. For some patients who were diagnosed as terminal, there were miraculous recoveries. For others, the technique failed. An important ingredient for success appeared to be a strong belief in the technique and a genuine desire for it to work. The imagery also had to be strong and positive. Images of sharks eating the cancer cells or of white knights on white horses charging through the landscape killing slow-moving creatures are examples of potent images.

The images used were either an accurate representation of the physiological processes involved or more fanciful representations. In an intriguing account, Shattock (1979) describes using visualiastion techniques to cure arthritis of the hip, an enlarged prostate gland and to remove a polyp from his nose. He researched the physiological processes involved in great detail and, as closely as possible, made his visualiastion an exact replication of the necessary healing process.

The idea that the use of imagery techniques can have an effect on our bodies to the extent of curing serious illness, even those diagnosed as terminal, has been strongly criticised in some quarters. Whatever the outcome of the medical debate, there does seem to be evidence that the technique has worked for some individuals. Indeed, there is a growing body of convincing evidence to suggest that a good proportion of illness is psychosomatic and that a neutral medication or placebo can cure patients if they believe it will work. This is not so far removed from the idea that the body can be cured by visualising the healing process. A further implication of these ideas is that imagery can be used to prevent illness by reducing stress levels and encouraging the positive image of a strong healthy body. Work is also being done in Australia on using visualisation techniques to help combat AIDS and prolong life expectancy for those with the virus.

RELAXATION

We have mentioned the link between imagery and relaxation several times. The exact physiological connections remain as yet unknown. The suggestion that both functions are mediated by the right side of the brain is an informed guess.

Approaches to relaxation are many and varied. Progressive relaxation involves tensing up and letting go the various muscle groups in turn. Autogenic training advocates making a series of suggestions to yourself, such as 'my right arm is warm and relaxed', and this is repeated with the appropriate phrases for different parts of the body. (See Mason, 1980, for a more detailed description of the many different approaches to relaxation.) Talking another person through a series of visual or other sensory images is in itself a relaxing process. The next set of scripts are specifically intended for healing or relaxation and would be appropriate to use with students involved in a programme of work around the theme of stress reduction and management.

Chapter Eleven

RELAXATION AND HEALING SCRIPTS

Teachers and students report schools as being highly stressful places. In any one school day hundreds of different interactions are taking place, some of which may be unresolved, leaving the participants in an emotional and stressed state. Teachers on in-service courses describe being 'drained' physically and emotionally at the end of a school day. A reasonable assumption would be that students share this feeling too. As parents we have noticed that our own children want to do little but watch television at the end of the school day and are virtually incommunicado while children's programmes are on. This is a not uncommon phenomenon and we believe one that provides an opportunity for children to withdraw into themselves after the stress of a school day.

Very little is done in schools to acknowledge the impact of such stressful interactions upon the learning process. Schools can even unwittingly induce a high state of arousal in both students and teachers, either by overstimulation of various kinds or as a result of boredom. Neither state is conducive for learning to take place. Teachers of primary-age students have long realised the need to have bursts of activity punctuated by periods of quiet during the school day and story time is a tried and tested method of calming and quietening younger students. Unfortunately, the rigidly structured timetable of most secondary schools militates against organising students' time in this way. We would suggest that scripted fantasy can provide a unique opportunity during the school day for students to withdraw temporarily from stressful interactions in a way that is both legitimate and educationally rewarding.

Structuring time to meet the appropriate physical and psychological requirements of students is particularly necessary for students with special educational needs. Elements that may characterise the behaviour of students across the range of special needs are many and diverse. Three behaviours relevant for this discussion are: first, a short attention span; second, daydreaming; and third, disruption in groups. The introduction of a periodic relaxation procedure followed by a scripted fantasy can help mitigate the need some students feel to withdraw from difficult situations into daydreaming or to indulge in acting out or disruptive behaviour. For both student and teacher there is the immediate reward of a significant reduction in stress and bodily tension which accompanies these activities. This may not happen the first time the technique is introduced to the group. Paradoxically, it is often the case that even though the group appeared to the teacher not to be relaxed, the feedback the students give is that they felt relaxed as a result of the activity.

Below we provide examples of scripts that are particularly conducive to generating relaxation.

THE RIVERSIDE

Water appears to be a particularly potent image for generating relaxation. This may have its origins in the amniotic fluid that warms and cushions the growing foetus in the mother's womb. Here the image of water is combined with a range of sensory experiences including warmth, which also plays an important part in the relaxation process.

Take two deep breaths and allow your body to relax.... Just let the tension go.... Imagine that you are sitting by a river on a warm summer's day.... Listen carefully and you can hear the sound of insects in the grass around you.... Hear the song of the birds in the trees in the distance.... You can smell the river water.... Listen to the gentle sound of the river as it moves along the bank near to you.... Watch the water as it gently laps by.... Dip your hand in and feel the temperature of the water.... Watch the patterns on the surface of the water.... In the distance you can see a leaf floating downstream.... Watch the leaf as it slowly floats past you.... Moves on and slowly floats away.... Lie back in the grass and enjoy the warmth of the sun and the coolness of the water.... Listen to its gentle lapping against the river bank.... Now in imagination, say goodbye to the riverside and as you begin to breathe a little more deeply, gently come back to the room.

THE SAND AND THE SEA

This is an example of a fantasy in which suggestions are contained within the body of the text – for example, 'You feel peaceful and comfortable' – in order to induce a greater sense of relaxation. As a general rule we would not encourage this interpolation into the students' own internal experience but feel it to be benign when used for the purpose of stress reduction.

Take two deep breaths and allow your body to relax.... Just let the tension go.... Now I want you to imagine that you are on a beach by the seaside on a warm, sunny day.... You are walking down the beach to the seashore.... You can hear the waves gently lapping against the sand.... Perhaps you can feel the rough sand with your bare feet.... You feel peaceful and comfortable.... Now you begin to heap up a mound of sand like a small sandcastle near the edge of the sea.... Take some time to build the mound and really enjoy the sensation of the damp sand in your hands.... Now stand back and take a look at what you have made.... As you stand, you can see a wave coming.... It's only a small wave.... It slowly washes up to you and gently laps against the edges of the mound and washes a small part of it away.... More waves, larger now, lap against the mound and slowly wash it away.... As you watch the final wave flowing back into the sea you can see that the sand is smooth and clean.... You might like to sit down and watch the waves lapping on the sand.... Watch the whitecaps far out at sea.... Let the feeling of relaxation wash over you.... As you slowly let the images fade stay with the feeling of relaxation.... When you are ready, breathe a little more deeply and take your time to come gently back to the room.

THE WATERFALL

In this script students are asked to make a strong identification with the image of the waterfall. The waterfall itself becomes a metaphor for the energy contained within the body which can simultaneously cleanse and relax. Identifying feelings that may be locked in stressed areas of the body is an important skill in releasing deep-seated muscular tension and the post-fantasy discussion might usefully focus upon how the students felt in their bodies during the experience.

> Take two deep breaths and let your body relax.... Just let the tension go.... Now I want you to imagine a waterfall.... Any waterfall that comes into your mind.... Just watch the waterfall for a while.... Become aware of how the water is falling over the rocks.... Look around now at the countryside.... See the spray thrown up by the falling water and the rainbow colours of the sun shining through the spray.... Listen to the sound of the waterfall as the water pours down.... Be aware of the smell and the taste of the water in the air thrown up by the spray.... How do you feel as you watch and listen?.... Now, in imagination, try to merge with the waterfall.... Try to become the waterfall.... Experience it as a bodily sensation right now.... Have the sense that the water is flowing down your face.... Down your arms.... Out through your fingers.... Have the sense that the water is flowing down your chest and down your back.... Down through your pelvis.... Down your legs and flowing out through your feet.... Feel the water flowing through you.... Moving down.... Moving downwards.... Feel the power and the energy moving through you.... Just enjoy the sensation for a while.... Now let that sensation go, and feeling relaxed and alert, come back to the room when you feel ready.

THE HAMMOCK

The rhythmic rocking of the hammock tends to induce a deep sense of peace and relaxation in the fantasiser. For many, rocking is a movement associated with feelings of calm and security clearly linked to early childhood experiences. It is this heightened state of relaxation that enables students to become more sensitive to the sensory experiences contained within the fantasy.

> Take two deep breaths and let your body relax.... Just let the tension go.... I want you to imagine that you are on a warm, tropical island.... You are lying in a hammock, strung be-

tween two palm trees.... Stare out to sea as you gently rock to and fro in the hammock.... Be aware of the texture of the material of the hammock as you rock.... What clothes are you wearing?.... Look up at the trees that are shading you from the hot sun.... How are you feeling as you lie there rocking?.... Listen to the sound of the sea gently washing against the sandy shore.... Hear the sound of the sea breeze moving through the branches of the trees.... Smell and taste the salt in the air as the breeze blows off the sea.... Just be aware of how you feel as you rock gently to and fro.... Close your eyes and just enjoy the sensation of having nothing to do right now.... Now become aware that it is nearly time to say good-bye to your tropical island.... But that you can bring the feeling of relaxation and well-being back to the room with you right now.

BUBBLES

Being caught up in a never-ending stream of worries, doubts and fears can produce high levels of stress and anxiety. For many students, these anxieties are centred around relationships with their families and their peers as well as problems associated with school work and the demands of examination syllabuses. This fantasy involves the fantasiser in briefly letting go of these distractions and thereby stilling the mind. This technique has its roots in meditation practices and offers students the opportunity first, to take a look at some of their immediate, pressing concerns, and second, to see how easy or difficult it is to let go of them.

Take two deep breaths and let your body relax.... Just let the tension go.... Now that you are relaxed and comfortable, just let a concern or worry in your life come into your mind.... Anything that is on your mind right now.... When it comes, imagine that it is being caught up in a bubble.... Now let the bubble gently float up out of your head.... Take a good look at the bubble as it hovers above your head.... Watch the bubble float away as it slowly rises up into the sky.... Let the bubble disappear off into the distance.... Now allow another concern to come into your mind.... Again allow it to float off in a bubble into the distance.... Do the same with all the

thoughts and worries that go around in your head.... You
may have several bubbles floating off at the same time....
Have the sense that your head is being emptied of thoughts
and worries.... You are just empty and still.... Try to keep this
sense of being empty of thoughts and worries as you breathe
a little more deeply and gently bring yourself back to the
room.

A DAY IN A BEAUTIFUL PLACE

Contemplation of natural beauty can be a relaxing, calming experience as well as being the forerunner to a discussion of aesthe-
tics. Many teachers find it difficult, even embarrassing, to introduce
the idea of beauty into the classroom, but this fantasy could be a
starting point for discussion. Students might subsequently be invited to bring in items they consider beautiful to continue the exploration.

Take two deep breaths and let your body relax.... Just let the
tension go.... Think of a beautiful place in the country.... It
could be in the mountains or by the sea, any place in the
countryside that seems beautiful to you.... It may be a place
you know or an imaginary place you would like to visit....
Make sure it is somewhere you can relax.... Now imagine you
are in this place and it is early morning, just before the sun
has come up.... Be aware of how you are feeling right here
and now.... Watch the sky begin to glow where the sun is
about to rise.... See the changing colours in the sky and the
scenery about you.... What are the sounds which you can hear
as the day begins?.... Now as time drifts by, you notice that
the sun is high in the sky, it is midday.... Be aware of the temperature of the air as it brushes against your skin.... What are
you doing now?.... Take in the sights and sounds and smells
and tastes.... Be aware of your body and how you are feeling.... Now imagine that time has drifted by and you are coming to the end of the day.... The shadows are getting longer....
The colours in the sky are changing.... The scenery looks different.... How are you feeling as the day draws to a close?....
The sun seems to become very large as it approaches the horizon.... The sounds around you start to change.... Just sit and

watch the sun as it gently moves down towards the horizon.... As the darkness begins to fall, realise that it is time to leave this beautiful place.... But that you can bring the feelings of peace and relaxation back to the room with you.... As you breathe a little more deeply and gently come back to the room.

THE CANDLE

The sensation of melting or letting go of tension tends to be associated with relaxation. In this script, the melting wax of the candle is related structurally to different parts of the body. This is similar to progressive relaxation, a technique that invites the participant to go systematically around the body and relax each part in turn. This ensures that the whole of the body is attended to and maximum relaxation achieved.

Sit up straight in your chair but try to be relaxed at the same time.... Take two deep breaths and allow your body to relax.... Have your feet flat on the floor and rest your hands on your legs.... Try to imagine that you are a candle.... Imagine that your head is the top of the candle.... In the centre of your head is a tiny flame which is completely enclosed in hard wax.... The flame is finding it hard to burn enclosed like this and sometimes it fades and almost burns out.... As the flame continues to burn, the wax above slowly begins to melt and become thinner.... This allows the flame to burn brighter and a small hole appears in the top of the candle.... As the wax continues to melt, light starts to stream out of the hole.... Have the sense that light is streaming out through the top of your head.... As the flame increases in strength, have the image that your forehead and the back of your head are melting.... The melting wax flowing down your arms and shoulders.... Your face and cheeks melting.... Now the wax around your shoulders begins to melt and dissolve.... Flowing down your neck and shoulders.... Continue with this sense of flowing and melting down the chest and the back.... Down the arms.... The flame of the candle glowing brightly, sending its light in all directions.... The body dissolving and melting.... Settling down to a soft melting pool on the floor.... Hold on to the feeling of softness and warmth and when you feel ready, let the images fade and gently come back to the room.

HEALTH SCRIPTS

Clinical research into the use of placebos in medicine has demonstrated the power of suggestion as a means of healing the body. In all of these trials doctors were perceived as medical experts who had the power and the means to heal. In the previous chapter, we discussed visualisation techniques as a means of enabling individuals to take more responsibility for monitoring their own health. By employing the technique of scripted fantasy, control over the healing process is in the mind and body of the fantasiser. What then has this to do with the classroom?

In schools, personal and social education programmes commonly embrace health education. Health educators are more and more seeking ways of encouraging students to take responsibility for their own physical and psychological well-being in order to increase awareness of the risks involved in alcohol, drug, solvent and sexual abuse, as well as a myriad of other self-destructive patterns. We would argue that scripted fantasy is one means of empowering students in relation to their own health. It is a method that harnesses the energy and the resources that each individual possesses to begin the healing process. Any healing that takes place could be psychological as well as physical; in fact, we would contend that the line between the two is blurred. It isn't necessary to be ill or injured to benefit from such healing suggestions.

REPAIRING THE BODY

In this fantasy the student is encouraged to evaluate for herself what repair is needed and to determine how that can best be achieved. The positive power of the individual over the process is emphasised throughout. This may not be an appropriate script for reinforcing learning about parts of the body as this might inhibit the more fantastic images that could emerge for some students.

Take two deep breaths and allow your body to relax.... Now imagine that you have become very small.... So small that you are in a tiny boat flowing along in the blood vessels of your

142

own body.... It doesn't matter how strange the images seem, just go along with them.... What does it look like inside your own veins and arteries?.... How do you feel about being here?.... Just go along with your journey in your tiny boat.... Have the sense that you are looking for parts of the body that need some healing.... When you reach a part of the body which is not quite right, find a way of getting out of the boat so you can have a closer look at what has happened.... Try to work out exactly what has gone wrong.... How do you think it could be repaired?.... Now go back to your boat and set off, in imagination, to a place in the body where there is an army of tiny workers who do repair jobs around the body.... What do they look like?.... Have a discussion with them about which part of the body needs repairing today and what needs to be done to it.... Set off with them to this place and help them with the repair work.... What do they do?.... What are you doing?.... When the work is completed, stand back and admire the handiwork.... Be aware of what you could do to prevent the damage happening again.... Now gently allow yourself to expand so that you merge with your real body and begin to come back to the room.

YOUR HEALTHY SELF

This fantasy centres around the notion of experiencing glowing health. By experiencing this feeling in imagination it is more likely that students will have an increased awareness of when their functioning is reduced by stress or disease. How can I know when I feel bad if I don't recognise when I am feeling good? This fantasy also promotes an awareness of body image, often a difficult subject for students to begin to discuss.

Take two deep breaths and allow your body to relax.... Just let the tension go.... Imagine that you are on a sandy beach.... You are with a group of people and you are playing a game.... What is the beach like?.... What is the weather like?.... What sort of game are you playing?.... Who are the people you are playing with?.... Now check that you aren't just watching yourself in the fantasy, but that you are actually in the fantasy and that you are looking at what is going on through your own eyes.... What is happening now?.... What can you hear?.... As you continue the game, have the sense that your body is strong and healthy and powerful.... Imagine your body is as healthy as you have ever known it to be.... You are relaxed and loose and breathing easily.... Be aware of the movememt of your limbs.... Feel the energy moving around your body.... You don't have to try to do anything.... Your body moves spontaneously.... Just go along with the movement and the feelings as the game continues.... Now you become aware that the fantasy is going to end soon and that you will be able to bring those feelings of health and vitality with you back to the room.... When it is right for you, breathe a little more deeply and gently come back to the room.

USING YOUR ENERGY

This fantasy focuses awareness on energy contained within the body and by visualising it, uses its power to heal. This has parallels in eastern forms of healing such as acupuncture, which is described as 'alternative' medicine and therefore in some way questionable. However, no one would deny that the notion of energy plays an important part in describing experience.

Find a comfortable place to sit or lie down.... For a moment just be aware of how you are breathing.... Just a gentle movement of the chest as the body breathes itself.... As you start to relax, the breathing begins to settle down.... Be aware of how warm or cold the temperature is and the feel of the air against your skin.... You might hear sounds outside the room and faint sounds from the other people in the room.... You might be aware of your heart beating and the pulses around your body.... As you continue to relax, you may feel a tingling sensation in parts of the body, particularly in the face and hands.... Imagine the tingling as energy moving around the body.... What does the energy look like?.... Try to visualise it.... See a picture in your mind of the energy.... See it moving around your body.... Have the sense of this energy moving down the arms and legs.... Around the chest and stomach.... Up into the head.... It is as if the whole of your body is being filled with energy.... As the movement of energy becomes stronger, it begins to vibrate.... There is an energy field which is moving inside and outside the body.... It is as if the body is enclosed in a field of vibrating energy.... The energy field begins to glow.... Now have the sense that you can concentrate the energy in a part of the body which is damaged or hurt in some way, or which you would like to change.... A part of the body which needs some healing or some extra attention.... Allow the energy to concentrate in that place and work in a way that is both helpful and healing to you.... Just let the energy work to your advantage.... When it is right for you, begin to come back to the room, but don't lose the sense of the energy moving around your body.... Now perhaps open your eyes and look around the room, but keep the awareness of the energy.

HEALING WATER

The therapeutic properties of water have been known for centuries. *Aqua vitae* – the water of life – is the agent for healing in this fantasy. It may also be a means of reducing anxiety about water for students who are reluctant to learn to swim.

Take two deep breaths and let your body relax.... Just let the tension go.... Imagine that you are standing by a pool of water which is deep enough to swim in.... The pool is filled by a hot spring which comes out of the ground.... Steam is rising from the surface of the hot water.... What can you see around the pool?.... Smell and taste the steam in the air.... What sounds can you hear in this place?.... How do you feel about being here?.... The water in the pool is famous for its healing qualities.... Build up the feeling that you are going to walk into the water and that this will be a safe thing to do.... How do you feel about the idea of walking out into the water?.... Now prepare yourself to get into the water.... Find a way of going down into the water, which is deep enough for you to stand up in.... Feel the warm water against your body.... See the steam rising up from the water around your head.... Have the sense of the healing qualities of the water soaking into your body.... What does this feel like?.... It is easy to float in the water, so you can lie back and float without any effort.... How does this feel?.... Relax in the warm water which is supporting you.... The healing qualities of the water start to soak into your muscles.... Releasing the tension in the muscles.... Be aware of the sense of healing soaking into the whole of the body.... Soaking through to the marrow of the bones.... Soaking through to the centre of every cell in your body.... The healing properties start to work on repairing any damaged parts of the body.... Gently repairing and healing.... Now begin to come back to the room, but keep the sense of the healing properties continuing to work inside your body.

HEALING DRINK

Another means of taking awareness and healing to different parts of the body is through the image of a healing drink that spreads feelings of well-being and vitality to different parts of the body. The idea of the magic potion with its powers to transform has long had a powerful grip on the public imagination. Here this image is used to promote positive feelings which are under the control of the fantasiser.

Take two deep breaths and let your body relax.... Just let the tension go.... Imagine you are sitting at a table.... There is a phial of golden liquid and an empty glass in front of you.... Build up the feeling as you look at it that the liquid has strong healing powers.... Now reach out and pick up the phial and examine it closely.... What shape is it?.... What is it made of?.... Now take the top off and pour some of the liquid into the glass.... Watch the liquid as you pour it into the glass.... Lift the glass to your lips and drink deeply.... What does it taste like?.... As the liquid pours down your mouth and throat, begin to feel a sense of well-being spreading through your body.... Feel the power of the liquid passing down your arms into the hands.... Down the legs and into the feet.... Up into the head.... Feel the sense of glowing vitality become stronger and stronger.... Enjoy the sensation and be aware that you will be able to keep this sense of glowing vitality for the rest of the day.... When you are ready, breathe a little more deeply and gently bring your awareness back to the room.

HEALING MASSAGE

There is evidence from research into biofeedback that it is possible to produce physiological changes in different parts of the body simply by attending to them. Lowering blood pressure would be an example of this. Relaxing the muscles in a specific part of the body results in an increased flow of blood, an important precondition for healing. Here the potency of the relaxation is increased by an imaginary massage.

Take two deep breaths and let your body relax.... Just let the tension go.... As the relaxation becomes deeper I want you to take your attention to your body.... Now focus your awareness on a part of the body that needs some attention.... Some healing.... It may be an old injury or a recent hurt or even a part of you that you feel needs some care.... Now, in imagination, I want you to massage the part that needs attention.... As you massage, try to have the feeling that you are putting care and attention into the massage.... Experience the massage as a bodily sensation.... As you continue to massage you might want to say a few words to the hurt.... It may want to reply.... Perhaps the hurt might tell you the best way of healing it.... Now get the feeling that there has been an improvement, that some healing has taken place and your massage has worked.... Finally, bring this sense of well-being with you as you breathe a little more deeply and come gently back to the room.

147

Chapter Twelve

HISTORICAL BACKGROUND

Many academic and experimental psychologists would claim that imagery and fantasy are not appropriate areas for psychological enquiry because they cannot be observed objectively. The researchers have to rely on self-report from subjects or examine their own internal experience. This has resulted in a dearth of writing by psychologists about scripted fantasy. There is very little rigorous, controlled research supporting the use of such techniques.

However, a clinician working with disturbed patients in a therapeutic setting cannot ignore the fantasies, delusions and daydreams of the patients because these often play an important part in the condition that is being treated. By the turn of the century, some psychiatrists had begun to use the material generated from patients' fantasies for diagnostic and therapeutic purposes. Ellenberger (1970) reviews the work and thinking of the time. Janet combined hypnosis with spiritist procedures such as automatic writing and crystal-gazing to generate images from his patients' unconscious. He suggested that these images were split-off parts of the personality that were not part of the patient's conscious experience. Having brought this material into consciousness, Janet tried to change or even eradicate it. Binet, the psychologist better known for his work on intelligence testing, was working along similar lines. He developed a technique that enabled his patients to talk to the visual images they produced. He then interpreted these images as the expression of unconscious personalities.

In his early work, Freud encouraged his patients to report their imagery aloud and would press his hand on their heads to encourage the process. His shift from the direct use of imagery to extended free association with the eyes open diminished the possible use of imagery, though his work with dreams is clearly related. Later psychoanalysts returned to an interest in the use of imagery in the therapeutic situation. In particular, Reyher (1963) developed images in the manner of Jung's 'active imagination', but interpreted the images within a Freudian psychoanalytic framework.

Jung (1875–1961) has probably had more influence than any other writer in developing an awareness of the power of imagery for understanding unconscious processes. After his breach with Freud, Jung went through a period of intense personal analysis. This included considerable experimentation with spontaneous activities, such as building sand castles, carving stone, painting mandalas and pictures, generating visual images and holding conversations with persons appearing in his imagination. He describes these activities as a 'confrontation with the unconscious' (Jung, 1961).

In contrast to Freud, Jung (1960) argued that the process of free association can be used as a means of avoiding important elements of dreams and fantasies. He stressed the importance of staying with the feelings associated with the images so that they can be properly understood. He argued that civilized life, which seems to place a high value on conscious, rational, directed thought processes, encourages the individual to be split off from or unaware of unconscious processes. However, the energy associated with the emotional aspects of these unconscious processes can easily break out, often with undesirable consequences. Working with imagery contributed to the unification of conscious and unconscious. Jung called this the 'transcendent function'.

Based on his own experience, Jung developed the technique of 'active imagination'. This was done by the patients themselves away from the consulting room. They were asked to re-experience aspects of dreams and fantasies, encounter and confront elements in them and engage them in conversations; in essence, to build up an ongoing dynamic relationship between the conscious and unconscious mind. This was described as confronting the unconscious while awake. It is similar to the techniques of *Gestalt* therapy, which we emphasised as an important technique for processing material produced from scripted fantasy work in the classroom.

The material generated by the patient was dealt with in a noninterpretative manner. Jung would ask questions like, 'What occurs to you in connection with that?', 'Where does that come from?', or 'How do you think about it?' – again, a mode of questioning similar to *Gestalt* therapy. The interpretations seemed to emerge of their own accord from the patient's replies and associations. Another aspect of Jung's view of dream and fantasy imagery is that it has an important creative function for the individual. It is this creative function that we emphasise as being a necessary part of the education process that can be harnessed by the use of scripted fantasy in schools.

This approach contrasts with the impression given by Freud that the unconscious is merely a sink for experiences, feelings, thoughts and infantile wishes that have traumatic and unpleasant associations for the adult client. Jung suggests that by looking at and concentrating on the images, they become pregnant with power, implying a purposive as well as a repressive function of the unconscious. He goes on to suggest that part of the creative function of the psyche is to provide a dynamic equilibrium for underdeveloped or missing parts of the personality. These other parts may represent aspects of the personality that are no longer accessible to the individual's awareness, or they may represent Jung's (1959) 'archetypes' which have developed in human racial history.

Jung's work and ideas have probably been the most important influence on later developments for fantasy and imagery in therapeutic situations. Other writers from the same period include Happich (1932), who suggested that it was important to encourage 'emergent images' in a relaxed state. He argued that working with and developing imagery was more important for personal change than the verbal abstractions that are used in Freudian free association. Happich would stimulate imagery by suggesting scenes for the client to visit in imagination. Caslant (1921) made specific use of ascent and descent in imaginary situations. He found that higher levels were generally associated with good feelings and lower levels with bad feelings. Drawing on the findings of Caslant, we advise against using fantasy scripts that involve descent, such as potholes, underground caverns and going down under the sea.

The importance of Caslant's ideas concerning ascent and descent were also stressed by Desoille (1966). He also found that descent was usually associated with negative feelings and often produced frightening images. Ascent was said to be associated with positive feelings and played an important part in the 're- education' process. He suggested that these feelings developed through association with the rising and setting sun. Another interesting assumption he makes is that for a right-handed person, movement to the left induces feelings about the past and movement to the right induces feelings about the future. This process is reversed in left-handed people.

Desoille (1966) developed the use of guided fantasy as a complete psychotherapeutic system, consisting of a series of fantasy trips, which he claimed were curative in their own right. The client would lie on a couch in a relaxed position. She or he would be given a starting theme and the therapist would ask questions in order to develop the fantasy. Frightening images that emerged during the fantasy journeys were focused on and worked with, to try to discover more about them and the root of the emotions associated with them. He assumed that this process of discovery would reduce the strength of the negative feelings. Specific stategies were offered to help the client cope with difficult emotional situations generated by the imagery, so that monsters could be tamed with the powers of a magic wand. This might be developed to suggest that the magic wand would transform the monster into a real person. Desoille sometimes found that the monster turned out to be a person close to and important in the client's emotional life. Another approach to a difficult situation in a fantasy journey was to ask the client to imagine being led by the hand by a real or imaginary trustworthy person. The guide again often turned out to be a person who was close to the client.

A similar psychotherapeutic system was offered by Leuner (1969), who gave his clients a series of ten standard imagery themes which he said represented different aspects of the client's inner life. He claimed that his first three themes – the meadow, climbing a mountain and following a stream, either up to its source or down to the ocean – tended not to produce frightening material. Certainly this is a view that the writers would take issue with from their own experience of working with these themes. Leuner claimed that these themes were used to help the client become more familiar with journeys in the imagination. He claimed that other themes, such as the fierce beast, the dark forest and the swamp, tended to produce material that was more difficult for the client to cope with emotionally.

Both Desoille and Leuner provided a clearly defined symbology for fantasy experience that imposed a structure and value on their clients' inner world which the clients did not necessarily share. The limitations of such interpretations are discussed in detail in Chapter Eight, 'Projection'.

These developments in psychotherapy, reviewed by Singer (1974), became more readily available to the general population through the system developed by the Italian psychiatrist Assagioli (1965) called psychosynthesis. He argued that treatment should go beyond analysis and extend to synthesis, which involved the development and integration of the whole of a person's potential. He used many techniques involving fantasy, ranging from visualisation of specific themes to extended imagery trips similar to those of Desoille and Leuner. Ferrucci (1982) provided good examples of the use of fantasy within this system.

Another development of the use of fantasy was within what has been described as 'the personal growth movement'. During the 1950s, 1960s and 1970s a range of experiential workshops were set up in order to help participants become more aware of themselves and how they related to others. What characterised the personal growth movement was that it made techniques previously available only to those who were defined medically as being mentally ill, accessible to a large section of the general 'healthy' population. Much of the work was developed out of a humanistic psychological tradition, which stressed the potential of all human beings to change and grow in positive ways (Rogers, 1983).

The facilitators of experiential personal growth workshops drew on a wide range of sources for their inspiration. It was this very eclecticism that allowed them legitimately to use imagery to enhance their repertoire of skills. This produced a subtle shift in emphasis from the use of fantasy to help a disturbed person attain 'normality', to using fantasy to help 'normal' people improve the quality of their lives. The role of facilitator itself contrasts starkly with that of the psychotherapeutic expert, and highlighted the debate about power and control in the learning situation. This approach helped to demythologise the notion of the medical expert and put power and responsibility for learning and living back into the hands of the learner. Again, forms of scripted or guided fantasy played an important part in these developments, often borrowing directly from psychosynthesis (Whitmore, 1986). Stevens's (1971) seminal work provided a useful source of fantasy scripts and important guidelines for the group facilitator.

Schools mirrored these developments with the call for greater equality of educational opportunity via comprehensive schooling and the formalising of pastoral care structures within schools to ensure the personal and social development of students as well as their academic and intellectual growth. Despite the heady idealism of these years, teachers with pastoral responsibility in schools very quickly felt the limitations that a rigid pastoral structure imposed and many voiced the conviction that it was necessary both to integrate personal and social learning into the school curriculum, and have as many members of staff as possible involved in the planning and implementation of such PSE work. In education, too, the concept of the role of teacher underwent a paradigm shift, from the arbiter of all learning in the classroom to someone who negotiated curriculum strategies with other members of a team to meet the perceived cognitive and affective needs of students. We would not claim that this description characterises the behaviour of all teachers in schools but that the general, accepted understanding of the teacher's role had broadened to encompass this paradigm, which in essence was similar to and paralleled the demythologising of the medical/psychological expert.

In this book we have shown that the use of scripted fantasy as a technique can enhance the skills repertoire of teachers across the curriculum. We have described the historical development of the use of imagery and fantasy in psychotherapeutic settings through to the introduction of these techniques in the classroom. We would claim that fantasy and imagery can play an important part in enabling teachers to move towards a teaching model that stresses the need to pay attention to all cognitive and affective aspects of students' development. It has often been claimed, though not always practised, that we are all teachers of PSE. Employing the methodology of scripted fantasy in the classroom can make this dream a reality.

Chapter Thirteen

SCRIPTS FOR ENCOURAGING CREATIVITY

In some senses the title of this chapter is misleading. We would argue that all of the scripts in this book encourage personal creativity, be it in the interior world of the imagination or in the reflecting, talking, writing or drawing that may follow the activity. Whether or not the split-brain hypothesis is an accurate portrayal of the underlying physiology, fantasy does appear to liberate creative processes within the individual. We hope that teachers using this book and trying out fantasy in the classroom will discover for themselves reserves of creativity that may previously have been neglected.

THE VOLCANO

One block to creativity is the fear of letting go and permitting the release of natural spontaneity. Part of this fear is centred around the anxiety of what might potentially be released. The volcano is a powerful image for a vast reserve of energy that can be discharged with explosive power. Going through the process of an eruption or discharge in fantasy can provide a way of exploring an extreme form of letting go safely. This imaginary form of letting go is often experienced as a release of energy in the body.

> Take two deep breaths and allow your body to relax.... Just let the tension go.... I want you to imagine that you are at the foot of a volcano.... Build up the feeling that you are going to climb up to the crater and have a look inside.... Begin your journey now and have a good look around you as you journey upwards.... What can you see?.... You are near the rim now.... The ground beneath your feet begins to vibrate and you can hear a dim rumble.... Wisps of smoke come over the

rim and you can smell the sulphur in the air.... Stand on the edge of the crater now and have a good look into the heart of the volcano.... What can you see?.... How are you feeling right now?.... See if there is anything you want to say to the heart of the volcano.... Now become the heart of the volcano.... What do you think of the person standing on your rim?.... What would you like to say back to this person?.... Just let the dialogue continue naturally.... Now realise that soon the volcano will erupt.... How do you feel about this?.... Go to a safe place to watch the eruption.... What can you see?.... What can you hear?.... How are you feeling?.... Just let the volcano do what it wants to do.... Now the eruption is dying down.... The earth gradually stops moving now.... As you watch, check out how you are feeling.... Now let the images fade and breathe a little more deeply.... When it is right for you, gently come back to the room.

Students put a great deal of energy into their subsequent drawings of the volcanic eruptions and they can also be encouraged to describe their feelings as they watched the volcano erupt.

PAINTBRUSH

Allowing students free access to their imaginations is a rare occurrence in many schools. Students' own creativity is restricted by the limits of the teacher's creativity or hidebound by instructions, syllabuses and rules. Creative imagining then by definition becomes contextual and bounded. This fantasy enables students to set the context for themselves and to explore the limits of their own imaginative capacity.

Take two deep breaths and allow your body to relax.... Just let the tension go.... Now imagine you are sitting at a table and on the table is a selection of paints, crayons, felt tips, pencils and other artist's materials.... Now build up a feeling that you are going to draw or paint on a large sheet of blank paper.... In imagination, pick up any of the artist's materials that seem right for you and draw or paint whatever comes.... Just let the picture come.... Take your time.... How do you feel about doing this?.... Take a good look at what you have drawn.... Now take the picture and give it as a gift to someone, anyone you choose.... How does the person react?.... How do you feel about giving that person your picture?.... When you are ready breathe a little more deeply.... Open your eyes and gently come back to the room.

Processing this fantasy through drawing will produce a broad range of different themes. A classroom display might provide the stimulus for a discussion on the power and individuality of the imagination and the appreciation of difference.

DANCING

The same exploration of the limits of creativity can be explored in this instance through the medium of an imaginary dance. The script can be modified to incorporate different rhythms or even accompanied by a particular piece of music. A discussion following the fantasy experience might explore the students' emotional and physical responses, or even attempt to recapture the fantasy in dance.

Take two deep breaths and allow your body to relax.... Just let the tension go.... I want you to imagine you are standing in a room on your own.... The room is empty and you are standing on a carpet in your bare feet.... Feel the carpet beneath your feet.... How do you feel right now?.... From a corner of the room you can hear some music.... Faintly at first and then becoming louder.... Listen to the music as it plays.... What is the melody like?.... What are the rhythms like?.... In the fantasy, close your eyes and permit your body to sway to the rhythm of the music.... How do you feel now?.... Allow the music to change and grow as it suits you.... Follow the sounds and rhythms with your whole body.... Begin to move around the room.... Now let the music and the dance go any way you want.... Allow the music and the dance to take control.... Have the sense of becoming one with the music as you follow it with your body.... Now the music begins to slow and becomes quieter.... Allow your dance to slow too and eventually stop.... The music slows and then stops.... How are you feeling now?.... Stay with these feelings as you gently begin to come back to the room.

YOUR DOOR

Opening doors can be construed as a metaphor for opening up possibilities where none previously seemed to exist. Learning how to open the door at will is an important aspect of encouraging creativity.

Take two deep breaths and allow your body to relax.... Just let the tension go.... I want you to imagine that you are wandering through a large building.... There are many twisting corridors with doors on each side.... The doors have people's names written on them.... Some of them are the names of people you know and are close to you.... Go up to some of the doors and read the names.... You try the door handles and find that they are securely locked.... How are you feeling right now?.... Carry on looking at the doors as you carry on down the corridor.... Suddenly you realise that the door you are looking at has your name on it.... How do you feel about this?.... What is the door like?.... Reach out and touch the door and feel its surface.... Build up the feeling that it is safe to open the door.... Now you take hold of the handle and try the door.... It is not locked; the handle turns and the door begins to open.... Go through the door and see what is on the other side.... Now let the fantasy go wherever it wants.... What is happening?.... How are you feeling?.... Just go along with the images that come.... Now let the fantasy fade and when it is right for you, breathe a little more deeply and begin to come back to the room.

SHAPING CLAY

Clay is a powerful medium for self-expression and working with it has therapeutic value as a stress-reducing activity. Teachers do not always have access to clay, but students always have access to their imaginations. In this fantasy clay can be substituted for play-dough, plasticine, building bricks or wood, with the appropriate modifications to the instructions. This script can be processed through drawing, or indeed clay, and the discussion might centre around the significance the object has for each student and what they chose to do with it.

157

Take two deep breaths and allow your body to relax.... Just let the tension go.... I want you to imagine that you are sitting at a table and on the table is a lump of clay.... How big is the lump of clay?.... Try reaching out and touching it.... What does it feel like?.... Do you like the texture?.... Is it warm or cold?.... Hard or soft?.... Now try kneading the lump of clay with both hands.... You can even hit it if you want to.... How are you feeling right now?.... Build up the feeling that you are going to make something with the clay.... Make something with it now.... Take your time and make something that feels right for you.... Now sit back and have a good look at what you have made.... How do you feel about your creation?.... What would you like to do with it now?.... Now let the images fade and begin to come back to the room.

THE FOUR SEASONS

The seasonal changes that mark each year provide a cogent metaphor for the ebb and flow of the creative impulse. For all of us there may be times when creativity seems to be blocked but an appreciation that everything is continually changing can have a subtly releasing effect on the imagination. This fantasy might serve as a powerful stimulus for poetry or descriptive prose with secondary or older primary-age students.

Take two deep breaths and allow your body to relax.... Just let the tension go.... In your imagination I want you to go to a place that you know very well.... Now imagine that it is springtime.... Look around.... What do you see?.... What can you hear?.... How can you tell it is springtime in this place?.... How are you feeling in this place in springtime?.... Build up the feeling that spring is going to change into summer.... How do you feel about the change?.... Look around.... What do you see?.... What can you hear?.... How can you tell it is summer in this place?.... How are you feeling in this place in summertime?.... Build up the feeling that the summer is going to change into autumn.... How do you feel about the change?.... Look around.... What do you see?.... What can you hear?.... How can you tell it is autumn in this place?.... How are you feeling in this place in autumn?.... Build up the feel-

158

ing that autumn is going to change into winter.... How do you feel about the change?.... Look around.... What can you see?.... What can you hear?.... How can you tell it is winter in this place?.... How are you feeling in this place in winter-time?.... Now I want you to let those images go and to choose the season of the year that you like best.... Spend some time exploring the sights and sounds and feelings that go with this season.... Let the images gently fade.... Breathe a little more deeply and when it feels right for you, come back to the room.

Chapter Fourteen

CONCLUSION

A growing number of teachers are already familiar with the use of scripted fantasy in the classroom. For others, the content of this book may seem far removed from the stuff of normal classroom activity. We would maintain that it is important to test out the effectiveness of experiential activities of this nature in order to understand the unique way in which imagery brings the students' experience of the world to the forefront of the learning process. It is important not to be put off by the initial difficulties that are in evidence when any new or 'different' activity is introduced into the classroom. We have indicated that the pay-off in using scripted fantasy can be considerable, not only in terms of the curriculum you teach, but also for the quality of the social climate in the classroom.

Throughout this book we have emphasised that scripted fantasy can be used with all age groups, all ability ranges and across the curriculum. The only limitation to the use of fantasy is the teacher's own creativity. For this reason we urge teachers to try out for themselves fantasy scripts before they attempt to use them with students, because it provides a means of liberating their own creative powers. We are not suggesting a swing totally in the direction of 'right-brain' activities in the classroom. Clearly this would be as distorted and as distorting as the current emphasis on 'left-brain' activities, such as cognition and reasoning.

The advantage that fantasy as a technique has over these more rational learning processes is that it is not dependent upon the normal stages of intellectual development for its effectiveness. The sophistication of the analysis of the fantasy experience will develop as the student matures emotionally and intellectually. For many people, emotional and intellectual development do not run in parallel. Highly academic adults may find personal relationships difficult and confusing, while some young children demonstrate an openness and self-awareness that is enviable. Using fantasy with people at each end of the construct continuum, from academic to emotional, can provide the means to explore and develop the potential for a fully integrated personality.

Teachers we have worked with over the past two decades report that using fantasy and imagery in the first instance as a means of self-exploration has enabled them to go on to develop their professional skills. This has come about through a change in perception of their role as educators. Developing new skills to accommodate the role of teacher as learner in collaboration with students brings with it the benefits of more open, caring and trusting relationships within the classroom.

Undoubtedly, the use of scripted fantasy is a break from the accepted, traditional approaches to classroom teaching. We would agree that some aspects of education involve the passing on of values and traditions of an existing culture and that this is an important function of education in all societies. However, schools should also be concerned with educating students to be capable of questioning the relevance of those traditions and values, to be open to change and capable of providing the impetus for future innovation and improvement within society. Such an education entails offering experiences that open up possibilities rather than close them down, that break out of existing routines and provide the potential for growth. Any system or institution which is not in a state of change, or indeed which cannot accommodate change, is unlikely to survive in a changing environment.

Change almost by definition involves risk, and risk may be associated with danger. Risk and danger raise the issue of the possibility of harming students by using scripted fantasy. We have no evidence of any psychological damage that can be attributed directly to using fantasy techniques. At worst, there may be initial complaints from students about wasting time, but this usually dissipates as the students come to a cognitive and affective understanding of the value of the experience. We have had no reports of complaints coming from parents, an anxiety that is often used to block innovative work in education. If the analyses by Holt (1964) and Hargreaves (1982) are correct, then conventional schooling practices are already doing considerable damage at both primary and secondary levels.

Cries of 'this is dangerous' are often applied to activities that run counter to the accepted strategies employed in the classroom. There seems to be an in-built resistance to activities that challenge existing prejudices and ways of thinking. Scripts that invite people to 'become' a member of the opposite sex or to change the colour of their skin can assist programmes designed to raise an awareness of sexism and racism. A white boy who has experienced in fantasy what it is like to 'be' a black girl, a wise person, a friend, a tree, or an animal in a cage may extend his capacity for empathic understanding. He may begin to accept that he can find solutions to his difficulties, recognise that he has both 'good' and 'bad' qualities, appreciate the feelings of another person and articulate his pain and anger, as well as his tenderness and joy.

It is understandable that some teachers are frightened by the intensity of the feelings that are expressed in the discussions, drawings and writing that follow scripted fantasy. There is sometimes a fear that it will not be possible to cope with the emotionality that may be triggered off. Only the experience of using fantasy in the classroom can allay such fears, but the fear must be measured against the reality that a small minority of students are acting out strong feelings in a negative and destructive manner on a daily basis in schools today. There is a strong possibility that scripted fantasy may provide a means of symbolising and working through these feelings which cannot always be dealt with explicitly or indeed be disclosed openly. Students can be given a range of scripted fantasies that enable them to express themselves in a way which overcomes blocks to communication. Through fantasy students are invited to discover the appropriate metaphor by which their unique response can be communicated to others.

We would go further and claim that it is only through metaphor that certain human experiences can be made sense of and communicated. Working with fantasy enables students to discover and share metaphors that are meaningful in their own lives. A world of experience lies open in which the boundaries of the imagination are unlimited and the student is free to explore. Diana Whitmore (1986), writing on psychosynthesis and education, claims that each person has within herself all she needs to grow and develop. If teachers superimpose their own pre-determined definitions of reality, the development of this potential is frustrated. By giving students the freedom to determine for themselves the content and meaning of experience in fantasy, teachers are positively encouraging students to trust their own judgement, to be confident of sharing their feelings, to trust and value others, acquire their own internal set of controls, take more responsiblity for their own lives and be clearer about their needs and values. In short, students can begin the difficult process of self-actualisation.

REFERENCES

Assagioli, R. (1965) *Psychosynthesis: A Manual of Principles and Techniques'* New York: Hobbs Dorman.

Bandler, R. and Grinder, J. (1979) *Frogs into Princes*, Moab, Utah: Real People Press.

Bartlett, F.C. (1932) *Remembering*, Cambridge: Cambridge University Press.

Blakeslee, T.R. (1980) *The Right Brain*, London: Macmillan.

Capra, F. (1982) *The Turning Point*, Hounslow: Wildwood House.

Caslant, E. (1921) *Methode de Developpement des Facultés Supranormales*, Paris: Edition Rhea.

Delaney, J. (1988) *Enhancing Classroom Climate*, unpublished B.Phil. dissertation, University of Nottingham.

De Mille, R. (1976) *Put Your Mother on the Ceiling*, Harmondsworth: Penguin Books.

Desoille, R. (1966) *The Directed Daydream*, New York: Psychosynthesis Foundation.

Ellenburger, H.F. (1970) *The Discovery of the Unconscious*, New York: Basic Books.

Ferrucci, P. (1982) *What We May Be*, Wellingborough: Turnstone.

Fugitt, E.D. (1983) *He Hit Me Back First*, Rolling Hills Estates, California: Jalmar Press.

Hall, E. (1983) 'Patterns of meaning in guided fantasy', *Journal of Mental Imagery*, 7 (1), 35–50

——— (1987) 'Fantasy in religious education: a psychological perspective', *British Journal of Religious Education* 10 (1), Autumn.

Hall, E. and Kirkland, A. (1984) 'Drawings of trees and the expression of feelings in early adolescence', British Journal of Guidance and Counselling 7, 1.

Hall, E. and Greenwood, E. (1986) 'The effects of fantasy on the expression of feeling and the quality of writing by young adolescents', in Russell, D.G., Marks, D.F. and Richardson, T.E. (eds), *Imagery 2*, Dunedin, New Zealand: Human Performance Associates.

Hall, E. and Hall, C. (1988) *Human Relations in Education*, London: Routledge.

Happich, C. (1932) 'Das Bildewusstein als ansatzestelle psychischer Behandlung', *Zentreblatt Psychtherapie* 5.

Hargreaves, D. H. (1982) *The Challenge for the Comprehensive School: Culture, Curriculum and Community*, London: Routledge.

Holt, J. (1964) *How Children Fail*, Harmondsworth: Penguin.

Johnson, V. (1978) 'Fun, fantasy and feeling', *Science and Children* 15 (4), 21–2.

Jones, A. (1986) *Making R.E. More Effective*, Nottingham: University of Nottingham, Religious Experience Research Project.

Joyce, B.R. (1984) 'Dynamic disequilibrium: the intelligence of growth', *Theory into Practice*, 23 (1), 26–34, Winter.

Jung, J.C. (1959) 'Archetypes and the collective unconscious', In *The Collected Works of C.J. Jung*, vol. 9. London: Routledge and Kegan Paul.

——— (1960) 'The transcendent function', in *The Collected Works of C.J. Jung*, vol. 8. London: Routledge and Kegan Paul.

——— (1961) *Memories, Dreams and Reflections*, Aneila Jaffe (ed.) New York: Random House.

Leuner, H, (1969) 'Guided affective imagery (GAI): a method of intensive therapy', *American Journal of Psychotherapy* 23 (1), 4–22.

Mason, L.J. (1980) *Guide to Stress Reduction*, Los Angeles: Peace Press.

Masters, R. and Houston, J. (1978) *Listening to the Body*, New York: Delacorte.

Oaklander, V. (1978) *Windows to Our Children*, Moab, Utah: Real People Press.

Ostrander, S. and Schroeder, L. (1979) *Superlearning*, New York: Souvenir.

Passons, W.R. (1975) *Gestalt Approaches in counselling*, New York: Holt, Rinehart and Winston.

Perky, C. W. (1910) 'An experimental study of imagination', *American Journal of Psychology*, 21, 422–52.

Reyher, J. (1963) 'Free imagery: an uncovering procedure', *Journal of Clinical Psychology* 19, 454–9.

Rogers, C.R. (1983) *Freedom to Learn for the Eighties*, London: Charles E. Merrill.

Shattock, E.H. (1979) *Mind Your Body*, London: Turnstone.

Simonton, O.C., Matthews-Simonton, S. and Creighton, J.L. (1980) *Getting Well Again*, New York: Bantam.

Singer, J.L. (1966) *Daydreaming and Fantasy*, London; George Allen and Unwin.

——— (1973) *The Child's World of Make-Believe*, New York: Academic Press.

——— (1974) *Imagery and Daydream Methods in Psychotherapy*, New York: Academic Press.

Sperry, R.W. (1968) 'Hemisphere deconnection and unity in conscious awareness', *American Psychologist* 23, 723–33.

Stevens, J.O. (1971) *Awareness: Exploring, Experimenting and Experiencing*, Lafayette, California: Real People Press.

Syer, J. and Connelly, C. (1984) *Sporting Body: Sporting Mind*, Cambridge: Cambridge University Press.

Whitmore, D. (1986) *Psychosynthesis in Education*, Wellingborough:

Turnstone Press.
Williams, M. (1985) 'School counselling and humanistic education', in Wooster, A.D. and Hall, F. (eds), *Human Relations Training in Schools*, Nottingham: University of Nottingham School of Education.

INDEX OF SCRIPTS

INDEX

DATE DUE